LET'S
EAT
Chinese

LET'S EAT

Chinese

Wendy Wei and Ku Yue-Mei

Editor
Wendy Hobson

foulsham
LONDON • NEW YORK • TORONTO • SYDNEY

foulsham
Yeovil Road, Slough, Berkshire, SL1 4JH

ISBN 0-572-01748-0

Photoset in Great Britain by Typesetting Solutions, Slough, Berks.
Printed in Great Britain by Cox & Wyman Ltd. Reading.

Contents

Introduction

In Chinese cuisine, rice and vegetables predominate, and soya beans provide a major source of protein. Meat, poultry and fish are less important than they are in many other cultures.

The Chinese adore food and spend many hours shopping for the finest ingredients then preparing and cooking them to perfection. The range of dishes is vast. They are also artistic in the presentation of their food, believing that food should appeal to more than just the sense of taste. In addition to having good flavour, the Chinese believe a dish should be fragrant, colourful and attractive. In a single meal, the various foods should have contrasting textures and the flavours should maintain a balance between strong and subtle, spicy and mellow.

A huge country, covering over nine million square kilometres in area, China's various regions differ widely in climate, terrain and natural resources. These differences determine what kinds of foods are available in a particular region and, as a result, influence the cooking style in that particular area.

The four main regional styles in China are : northern (including Peking, Shantung and Honan); coastal (Shanghai and Fukien); inland (Szechuan and Yunnan); and southern (Canton).

The northern region is relatively cold, and wheat, rather than rice, is the staple food. Most of the dishes are light and delicate. Garlic and spring onions are popular flavourings and spices, when used, are mild. Noodle dishes, steamed breads and dumplings are typical.

In the coastal region, of course, there are many fish and seafood recipes as well as many soups, especially delicious, clear, light soups. Dishes from this region are usually well seasoned with soy sauce, especially meat and poultry dishes.

The inland region is hot and almost tropical. Strongly seasoned, spicy foods are favoured here and one of the most popular seasonings is Szechuan pepper, much more potent than the black pepper more commonly used in Europe. Many dishes also call for deep frying.

The Chinese foods most familiar to Europeans come from the southern region surrounding Canton. Dishes characteristic of the Cantonese style are light, mildly seasoned and less greasy than those of the other three regions. Soy sauce, fresh ginger root, rice wine and chicken stock are the most frequently used seasonings. The people in this region prefer to taste the natural flavours of the main ingredients of a recipe rather than added spices. Many Cantonese dishes are prepared using the quick-cooking technique of stir-frying.

In this book, we have made a selection of tasty and varied Chinese dishes from all the regions so that you can savour some of the style and tastes of the best of Chinese cooking.

Ingredients

All the ingredients in the recipes are readily available in supermarkets, delicatessens or Chinese supermarkets. Where ingredients used are less common, a simple alternative is suggested.

Bamboo Shoots
These tender, ivory-coloured shoots of tropical bamboo plants are used separately as a vegetable and also to add crispness and a slight sweetness to dishes. They are available in cans and should be rinsed and drained before using.

Bean Sprouts
Small and white, these are the shoots of the mung bean plant. They are used separately as a vegetable and included in a wide variety of dishes. They are available fresh or canned, and should be rinsed in water before using. They can be stored in a bowl of water in the refrigerator.

Black Beans, Fermented
Black beans are strongly flavoured, preserved, small black soya beans. They are quite salty and are often used as a seasoning in combination with garlic. Fermented black beans are available in cans, bottles or plastic bags. They should be rinsed or soaked before using.

Chinese Cabbage
This is a tender vegetable with white stalks and green, crinkled leaves which is frequently included in soups and stir-fried dishes. It requires very little cooking.

Coriander
Sometimes called Chinese parsley, fresh coriander is a strongly flavoured green herb with flat leaves. It is commonly used as a seasoning or garnish. It is readily available in supermarkets.

Chilli Sauce
Made from crushed chilli peppers and salt, this sauce is available in cans or bottles. It is a bright red, hot sauce and should be used sparingly.

Five-Spice Powder
A blend of anise seed, fennel, clove, cinnamon and ginger or pepper, five-spice powder has a slightly sweet, pungent flavour and should be used sparingly.

Ginger Root
Ginger root is knobby, gnarled root with a brown skin and a whitish or light green inside. It has a fresh pungent flavour and is used as a basic seasoning in many Chinese recipes. Ginger root is readily available in supermarkets or greengrocers and will keep for weeks in the refrigerator if well wrapped. Simply peel the root and slice or grate it, as indicated in the recipe. Ground ginger is not an adequate substitute.

Hoi Sin Sauce
Made from soya beans, flour, sugar, spices, garlic, chilli and salt, this thick dark brown sauce adds a sweet, spicy flavour to many Chinese dishes.

Lychees
Lychees are small, juicy oval fruits with a bumpy reddish skin and white flesh. They are used in many dishes or served separately as a dessert. They are available fresh or stoned in cans, usually in a syrup.

Monosodium Glutamate
This is a flavour-enhancer made from dried fermented soya bean protein which is used in some Chinese foods. It can have unpleasant side-effects, however, such as headaches, and is not used in any of the recipes in this book.

Mushrooms, Dried
Chinese dried mushrooms are available in delicatessens

and Chinese supermarkets. They have a strong, distinctive flavour and are used in a variety of dishes. They must be soaked in boiling water before use and are usually sliced before cooking. Fresh mushrooms can be substituted, but will not give the same flavour and texture.

Noodles, Egg

Chinese egg noodles are thin pasta usually made of flour, egg, water and salt. They can be bought fresh or dried and can be boiled, braised, stir-fried or deep-fried. Cooking times vary between types of noodles so check the packet before cooking.

Noodles, Transparent

Sometimes called cellophane noodles, these are dry, hard, white fine noodles made from mung beans. They have little flavour of their own but readily absorb the flavours of other foods. They are available in packets and are used in many steamed, simmered, deep-fried or stir-fried dishes.

Oyster Sauce

This is a thick, brown concentrated sauce made of ground oysters, soy sauce and brine. It is used frequently in Cantonese dishes.

Peanut Oil

Peanut oil is golden in colour and has a light and slightly nutty flavour. It can be heated to high temperatures so is ideal for stir-fried dishes.

Plum Sauce

This thick, chutney-like sauce is often served with duck or pork dishes.

Satay Sauce

Made of soy sauce, ground prawns, chillies, sugar, garlic, oil and spices, satay sauce is hot and spicy and used to season meats.

Sesame Oil
Made from toasted sesame seeds, sesame oil has a strong, nutty flavour and is best used sparingly. It is generally used as a seasoning rather than a cooking oil.

Soy Sauce
This pungent, brown, salty liquid is made from fermented soya beans, wheat, yeast, salt and sometimes sugar. It is used as a seasoning and colouring. Light and dark sauces are available.

Spring Onions
Spring onions are used frequently in Chinese cooking. The green tops are also often curled and used as a garnish. To make spring onion curls, trim the onions at the point where the stem begins to turn green and reserve the bulbs to use in a recipe. Trim the green stems to about 10 cm/4 in. Using sharp scissors, cut each section lengthways into about 8 thin strips down to the beginning of the stem. Place the green onions in a bowl of cold water and add some ice cubes. Refrigerate for about 1 hour until the onions curl then drain and use as a garnish.

Spring Roll Wrappers
Commercially prepared dough is available to make spring rolls. It is rolled very thinly and cut into squares. Filo pastry can also be used.

Szechuan Pepper
This pepper comes from the inland Szechuan province and is the main reason why the food from that region is so hot. It is sold whole or crushed in small packets and should be used sparingly.

Tofu
Tofu or bean curd is used as a vegetable and as an excellent source of protein. It can be used in all kinds of recipes as it absorbs the flavours of other foods. It is available fresh or canned.

Water Chestnuts

These are served separately as a vegetable or used to add a crisp texture and a delicate sweet flavour to other dishes. They are available fresh or canned. Canned water chestnuts should be rinsed and drained before use.

Wuntun Skins

These are sold fresh or frozen in Chinese supermarkets in packets of about 30. Thaw frozen skins thoroughly before use.

Equipment

A reasonably equipped kitchen usually contains more than enough utensils to handle Chinese cooking. However, one item you may not have but may wish to consider purchasing is a wok, especially if you plan to make stir-fried dishes frequently.

Woks

Invented many centuries ago, the wok is an all-purpose cooking pan used in virtually every Chinese household for almost every kind of cooking. Traditionally, a wok was made from thin, tempered iron and had a rounded bottom for fast, even conduction of heat. Some woks are, of course, still made that way, but they have been adapted to use modern materials and to suit modern cookers.

Most woks are made of steel or aluminium and have a slightly flat bottom which is better on a gas or electric stove. Woks are also available with a non-stick surface. Some have a long wooden handle instead of the traditional thin metal handles on the sides. This eliminates the necessity of using pot holders.

Woks range in size from 30 to 60 cm/12 to 24 in in diameter, but a 35 cm/14 in wok is a good choice for most people as it can be used for most dishes without interfering with the use of other burners on the stove.

Before using a metal wok, it should be washed and seasoned. Wash it thoroughly in hot, soapy water and use a scouring pad if necessary to remove any protective coating. Rinse well with water and dry the wok thoroughly. Rub 15ml/1 tbsp of vegetable oil over the interior of the wok and place it over a low heat for about 5 minutes until it is hot. Remove from the heat and allow to cool.

After use, a wok should be soaked in hot water and cleaned with a sponge. Do not clean the wok with soap or scouring pads. Rinse the wok with water, dry it and place it

over a low heat until all the water evaporates. Then rub
5ml/1 tsp of vegetable oil over the inside of the wok to
prevent it from rusting.

Bamboo Steamers
Bamboo steamers are used inside a wok or other pan for
steaming a variety of ingredients. The advantage of the
traditional Chinese design is that they have a tightly fitting
lid to prevent the steam from escaping and they can be
stacked to cook a variety of ingredients at the same time.

Cleaver
Though not essential, a cleaver is another useful utensil for
Chinese cooking. It is handy for slicing, chopping and
mincing ingredients and is especially helpful for chopping
whole chickens and ducks into Chinese-style serving
pieces.

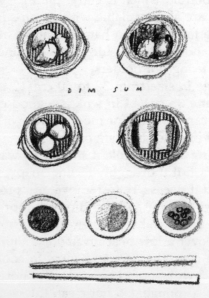

DIM SUM

Cooking Methods

Blanching
Foods are sometimes blanched in hot oil or water for a few minutes to cook them partially, ready for the final cooking with other ingredients. The food is then rinsed in cold water to stop the cooking process.

Braising
Many Chinese dishes, especially meat dishes, are slow-cooked in liquid. This gives tougher cuts of meat a long, slow tenderising process of cooking.

Stir-Frying
One of the most famous of Chinese techniques, stir-frying is best done in a wok to maintain the necessary high heat and thus enable you to stir the ingredients constantly while they are cooking. Always heat the oil almost to smoking point before you flavour it and add the ingredients.

Steaming
Chinese foods are often steamed to bring out the most delicate flavours. Bamboo steamers are the best utensils to use, but you can use a plate on a rack in a wok or saucepan.

Notes on the Recipes

1.   Follow one set of measurements only, do not mix metric and Imperial.

2.   Eggs are size 2.

3.   Wash fresh produce before preparation.

4.   Spoon measurements are level.

5.   Adjust seasoning and strongly flavoured ingredients, such as onions and garlic, to suit your own taste.

6.   If you substitute dried for fresh herbs, use only half the amount specified.

Regional Styles

Appetisers

It is best to serve a selection of appetisers to start a Chinese meal so that guests can choose a little of each dish. Essentially light and delicious, they are perfect for whetting the appetite for what is to follow.

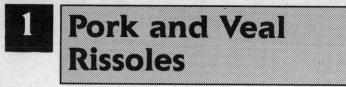

1 Pork and Veal Rissoles

Ingredients

100 g/4 oz minced pork
100 g/4 oz minced veal
1 slice streaky bacon, minced
5 ml/1 tsp soy sauce
Salt and freshly ground black pepper
1 egg
1 beef stock cube
30 ml/2 tbsp cornflour
Oil for deep-frying

Method

1. Mix together the pork, veal, bacon and soy sauce and egg and season to taste with salt and pepper. Break up the stock cube and sprinkle over the meat mixture.

2. Shape the mince into small balls and dust lightly with cornflour.

3. Deep-fry in hot oil for about 5 minutes until golden brown and drain on kitchen paper.

Serves 4

2 Dim Sum

Ingredients

100 g/4 oz peeled prawns, finely chopped
225 g/8 oz lean pork, finely chopped
50 g/2 oz cabbage, finely chopped
3 spring onions, finely chopped
1 egg, beaten
20 ml/4 tsp cornflour
10 ml/2 tsp soy sauce
5 ml/1 tsp sesame oil
5 ml/1 tsp oyster sauce
24 wuntun skins
750 ml/1 ¼ pts/3 cups vegetable oil

Method

1. Mix together the prawns, pork, cabbage and spring onions. Mix in the egg, cornflour, soy sauce, sesame oil and oyster sauce.

2. Working with about 12 skins at a time to avoid them drying out, place spoonfuls of the mixture on to the centre of each wuntun skin. Gently press the wrappers around the filling, tucking the edges together but leaving the tops open.

3. Heat the oil in a wok over a high heat until very hot. Fry a few dim sums at a time until golden. Drain on kitchen paper and serve hot.

Makes 24

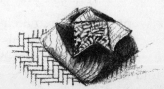

3 Pork and Prawn Wuntuns with Sweet and Sour Sauce

Ingredients

For the sauce:
120 ml/4 fl oz/½ cup water
60 ml/4 tbsp white wine vinegar
60 ml/4 tbsp sugar
30 ml/2 tbsp tomato purée
10 ml/2 tsp cornflour
25 g/1 oz mushrooms, finely chopped
25 g/1 oz peeled prawns, finely chopped
50 g/2 oz lean pork, finely chopped
2 spring onions, finely chopped
5 ml/1 tsp soy sauce
2.5 ml/½ tsp grated ginger root
½ clove garlic, crushed
24 wuntun skins
375 ml/13 fl oz/1 ½ cups vegetable oil

Method

1. Mix together the water, wine vinegar, sugar, tomato purée and cornflour in a small saucepan. Bring to the boil over a medium heat, stirring continuously. Simmer for 1 minute, stirring, then remove from the heat and keep the sauce warm.

2. Mix the mushrooms with the prawns, pork, spring onions, soy sauce, ginger and garlic.

3. Cut the wuntun skins into 8 cm/3 in circles using a biscuit cutter. Place spoonfuls of the pork mixture on to each circle, brush the edges with water, fold in half and seal the edges together.

4. Heat the oil in a wok over a high heat until very hot. Fry the wuntuns a few at a time for about 3 minutes until golden. Drain on kitchen paper and serve hot with the sweet and sour sauce.

Makes 24

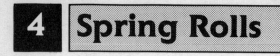

4 Spring Rolls

Ingredients

450 g/1 lb peeled prawns, finely chopped
450 g/1 lb lean pork, finely chopped
100 g/4 oz mushrooms, finely chopped
8 spring onions, finely chopped
1 red pepper, seeded and finely chopped
100 g/4 oz Chinese cabbage, finely chopped
225 g/8 oz/1 cup water chestnuts, finely chopped
45 ml/3 tbsp rice wine or dry sherry
15 ml/1 tbsp soy sauce
10 ml/2 tsp grated ginger root
5 ml/1 tsp sugar
2.5 ml/½ tsp salt
60 ml/4 tbsp water
15 ml/1 tbsp cornflour
24 spring roll wrappers
750 ml/1 ¼ pts/3 cups vegetable oil

Method

1. Mix together the prawns, pork, mushrooms, spring
    onions, pepper, cabbage, water chestnuts, wine or
    sherry, soy sauce, ginger, sugar and salt. Blend the
    water and cornflour until smooth.

2. Place 60 ml/4 tbsp of the pork mixture evenly
    across the corner of each spring roll wrapper.
    Brush the cornflour mixture evenly over the edges
    of the wrappers and roll the wrapper around the
    filling, folding in the corners.

3. Heat the oil in a wok over a high heat until very
    hot. Fry a few rolls at a time for about 5 minutes
    until golden. Drain on kitchen paper and serve hot.

Makes 24

5 Pork and Lettuce Rolls

Ingredients

25 g/1 oz dried mushrooms
15 ml/1 tbsp vegetable oil
225 g/8 oz lean pork, finely chopped
100 g/4 oz/½ cup bamboo shoots, finely chopped
100 g/4 oz/½ cup water chestnuts, finely chopped
6 spring onions, finely chopped
175 g/6 oz canned crabmeat, drained and flaked
30 ml/2 tbsp rice wine or dry sherry
15 ml/1 tbsp soy sauce
10 ml/2 tsp oyster sauce
10 ml/2 tsp sesame oil
9 iceberg lettuce leaves

Method

1. Soak the mushrooms in boiling water for 30 minutes. Drain and squeeze out any excess moisture. Remove and discard the stems. Finely chop the caps.

2. Heat the oil in a wok over a high heat. Stir-fry the pork for 6 minutes until golden. Add the mushrooms, bamboo shoots, water chestnuts, spring onions and crabmeat and stir-fry for 1 minute.

3. Mix together the wine or sherry, soy sauce, oyster sauce and sesame oil. Stir into the pork mixture and remove from the heat.

4. Place spoonfuls of the pork mixture on the centre of each lettuce leaf. Fold the ends and sides of the leaves over the filling and roll up to serve.

Makes 9

Stuffed Mushroom Caps

Ingredients

450 g/1 lb mushrooms
175 g/6 oz lean pork, finely chopped
50 g/2 oz/¼ cup water chestnuts, finely chopped
3 spring onions, finely chopped
½ small red or green pepper, finely chopped
1 stick celery, finely chopped
5 ml/1 tsp grated ginger root
5 ml/1 tsp cornflour
10 ml/2 tsp rice wine or dry sherry
5 ml/1 tsp soy sauce
2.5 ml/½ tsp hoi sin sauce
1 egg white
50 g/2 oz/½ cup plain flour
750 ml/1 ¼ pts/3 cups vegetable oil

For the batter:
50 g/2 oz/½ cup cornflour
50 g/2 oz/½ cup plain flour
7.5 ml/1 ½ tsp baking powder
5 ml/1 tsp salt
75 ml/5 tbsp milk
75 ml/5 tbsp water

Method

1. Remove and chop the mushroom stems and place them in a large bowl with the pork, water chestnuts, onions, pepper, celery and ginger.

2. Mix together the cornflour, wine or sherry, soy sauce, hoi sin sauce and egg white and stir into the vegetables. Spoon the mixture into the mushroom caps and dip the mushrooms in flour.

3.   Heat the oil in a wok over a high heat until very hot.

4.   Whisk together the batter ingredients. Dip the mushrooms in the batter, coating them completely. Fry a few at a time in the hot oil for about 5 minutes until golden. Drain on kitchen paper and serve hot.

Makes 24

7 Prawn Crackers

Ingredients

750 ml/1 ¼ pts/3 cups vegetable oil
100 g/4 oz prawn crackers

Method

1.   Heat the oil in a wok over a high heat until very hot.

2.   Add a handful of prawn crackers and fry for a few seconds until they have puffed up. Remove from the wok and drain on kitchen paper while you fry the remainder.

Serves 4

8 Fried Wuntuns

Ingredients

15 g/½ oz dried mushrooms
225 g/8 oz lean pork, finely chopped
50 g/2 oz spinach, finely chopped
22 ml/1 ½ tbsp rice wine or dry sherry
20 ml/4 tsp soy sauce
Freshly ground black pepper
24 wuntun skins
90 ml/6 tbsp pineapple juice
60 ml/4 tbsp white wine vinegar
10 ml/2 tsp tomato ketchup
50 g/2 oz/¼ cup sugar
30 ml/2 tbsp water
10 ml/2 tsp cornflour
60 ml/4 tbsp Chinese Mixed Pickles (page 126)
750 ml/1 ¼ pts/3 cups vegetable oil

Method

1. Soak the mushrooms in boiling water for 30 minutes. Drain and squeeze out any excess moisture. Remove and discard the stems. Chop the caps.

2. Mix together the mushrooms, pork, spinach, wine or sherry and half the soy sauce and season to taste with pepper.

3. Place spoonfuls of the mixture on to the centre of the wuntun skins. Gather the edges of the skins around the filling, pressing the tops firmly to seal.

4. Mix together the pineapple juice, wine vinegar, tomato ketchup, sugar and remaining soy sauce in a small saucepan. Bring to the boil. Blend the water and cornflour and stir into the mixture.

Simmer for 3 minutes. Stir in the mixed pickles and keep the sauce warm.

5.   Heat the oil in a wok over a medium heat until hot. Fry a few wuntuns at a time for 3 minutes until golden. Drain on kitchen paper. Pour over the pineapple sauce and serve.

Makes 24

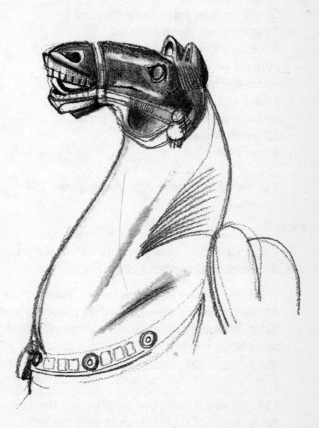

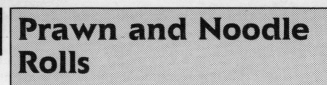

9 | Prawn and Noodle Rolls

Ingredients

50 g/2 oz/¼ cup egg noodles, broken into 2.5 cm/1 in
pieces
15 ml/1 tbsp butter or margarine
50 g/2 oz lean pork, finely chopped
3 mushrooms, finely chopped
3 spring onions, finely chopped
100 g/4 oz peeled prawns, finely chopped
½ hardboiled egg, finely chopped
15 ml/1 tbsp rice wine or dry sherry
Salt and freshly ground black pepper
20 wuntun skins
1 egg, beaten
750 ml/1 ¼ pts/3 cups vegetable oil
1 quantity Sweet and Sour Sauce (page 154)

Method

1. Cook the noodles according to the directions on
    the packet. Drain and chop finely.

2. Heat the butter in a wok over a medium heat and
    fry the pork for about 5 minutes until browned.
    Add the mushrooms and onions and stir-fry for 2
    minutes, then remove from the heat and mix in
    the prawns, hardboiled egg, noodles and wine or
    sherry and season to taste with salt and pepper.

3. Place spoonfuls of the mixture on the centre of
    each wuntun skin. Brush the edges lightly with
    beaten egg, roll up the wrappers tightly around the
    filling, pinching the ends slightly to seal.

4.   Heat the oil in a wok over a high heat until very
        hot. Fry the rolls a few at a time for about 5
        minutes until golden. Drain on kitchen paper and
        serve hot with sweet and sour sauce.

Makes 20

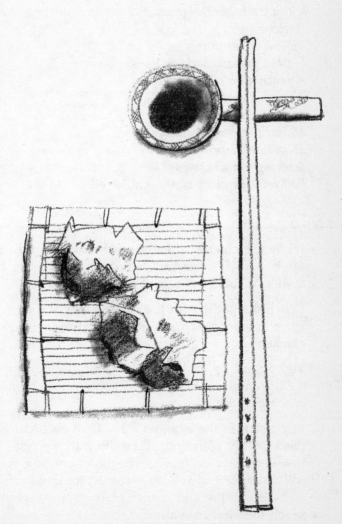

10 Ham and Chicken Rolls

Ingredients

2 chicken breasts, skinned
½ clove garlic
2.5 ml/½ tsp salt
Freshly ground black pepper
A pinch of five-spice powder
4 slices cooked ham
1 egg, beaten
30 ml/2 tbsp milk
25 g/1 oz/¼ cup plain flour
4 spring roll wrappers
750 ml/1 ¼ pts/3 cups vegetable oil

Method

1. Halve the chicken breasts and remove and discard the bones, if necessary. Pound the meat using a mallet or rolling pin until it is very thin.

2. Crush the garlic with the salt, pepper and five-spice powder and sprinkle the mixture over the chicken.

3. Tightly roll up each ham slice and place on top of a chicken piece. Roll the chicken around the ham, tucking in the ends.

4. Mix together the egg and milk. Coat each chicken piece lightly with flour, then dip into the egg-milk mixture. Place each piece diagonally on to a spring roll wrapper and roll up securely, folding in the ends. Brush the end corner with egg mixture and pinch together to seal.

5.   Heat the oil in a wok over a high heat until very
     hot then fry the rolls a few at a time for about 5
     minutes until golden and cooked through. Drain
     on kitchen paper. Cool slightly and cut into thick
     diagonal slices to serve.

Makes 4

11 Spicy Baked Tenderloin

Ingredients

30 ml/2 tbsp soy sauce
15 ml/1 tbsp dry red wine
10 ml/2 tsp brown sugar
10 ml/2 tsp honey
5 ml/1 tsp red food colouring (optional)
A pinch of ground cinnamon
1 clove garlic, crushed
1 spring onion, halved
1 pork tenderloin, trimmed
8 Spring Onion Curls (page 11)

Method

1. Mix together all the ingredients except the meat and spring onion curls in a large bowl. Add the pork, turning to coat it completely, then cover and refrigerate overnight, turning occasionally.

2. Drain the pork, reserving the marinade. Place the pork on a wire rack over a baking dish. Bake in a preheated oven at 180°C/350°F/gas mark 4 for 45 minutes, turning and basting with the marinade frequently.

3. Remove the pork from the oven and leave to cool. Cut into diagonal slices and serve garnished with spring onion curls.

Serves 4

12 Banana and Chicken Fries

Ingredients

2 cooked chicken breasts
2 firm bananas
4 eggs
120 ml/4 fl oz/½ cup milk
6 slices white bread, crusts removed and quartered
50 g/2 oz/½ cup plain flour
225 g/8 oz/4 cups soft fresh breadcrumbs
750 ml/1 ¼ pts/3 cups vegetable oil

Method

1. Skin and bone the chicken breasts and cut into 24 pieces in all. Peel the bananas and cut lengthways into quarters. Cut each quarter into thirds to give 24 pieces in all.

2. Beat the eggs and milk and brush the mixture over one side of the bread pieces. Place one piece of chicken and one piece of banana on the egg-glazed side of each bread piece.

3. Coat each square lightly in flour, then dip in the egg mixture and coat with breadcrumbs. Dip again into the egg, then the breadcrumbs.

4. Heat the oil in a wok over a high heat until very hot. Fry a few squares at a time for about 3 minutes until golden. Drain on kitchen paper and serve hot.

Makes 2

Soups

Chinese soups are delicious
combinations of fresh ingredients
in a tasty stock. Some are served
like a fondue, and used to cook
meat, fish or vegetables at the
table.

1 Chicken Stock

Ingredients

1 chicken carcass
6 green peppercorns
1 onion, quartered
½ turnip, cut into chunks
2 sticks celery, cut into chunks
1 large carrot, cut into chunks
1 x 2.5 cm/1 in piece ginger root

Method

1. Place all the ingredients in a large saucepan and just cover with water. Bring to the boil, cover and simmer for 1 hour. Leave to cool.

2. Skim any fat from the surface and bring to the boil again. Strain the stock and use as required.

    Makes about 2.5 litres/4½ pints/1 cup

Chicken and Sweet Corn Soup

You can use any kind of chicken pieces for the stock. There should be about 100 g/4 oz of chicken meat to add to the soup.

Ingredients

1 litre/1 ¾ pts/4 cups water
750 g/1 ½ lb chicken
4 whole peppercorns
5 ml/1 tsp salt
1 sprig of fresh parsley
1 onion, sliced
2.5 cm/1 in piece ginger root, thinly sliced
6 spring onions
350 g/12 oz creamed sweet corn
1 chicken stock cube
5 ml/1 tsp sesame oil
Freshly ground black pepper
30 ml/2 tbsp cornflour
1 egg white
25 g/1 oz cooked ham, cut into thin strips

Method

1. Place the water, chicken, peppercorns, salt, parsley and onion in a large saucepan. Reserve 2 slices of ginger and add the remainder to the pan. Bring to the boil, cover and simmer for 1 ½ hours. Skim any scum from the top and strain the stock. Return the stock to the pan. Shred the chicken meat and reserve about 100 g/4 oz.

2. Finely chop 4 of the spring onions and grate the reserved ginger. Add these to the stock with the sweet corn, stock cube and sesame oil and season to taste with salt and pepper. Bring to the boil.

3. Blend the cornflour with a little water and stir it into the stock. Simmer, stirring, until the stock thickens.

4. Beat the egg white with 30 ml/2 tbsp of water and drizzle it into the stock, stirring vigorously. Stir in the ham and reserved chicken and heat through.

5. Cut the reserved spring onions into thin strips. Pour the soup into bowls and garnish with the spring onions.

Serves 4

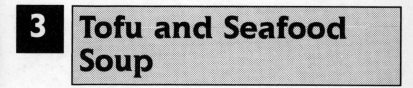

3 Tofu and Seafood Soup

Ingredients

1 litre/1 ¾ pts/4 ¼ cups chicken stock
225 g/8 oz/1 cup tofu, cubed
100 g/4 oz crabmeat
100 g/4 oz shelled prawns
100 g/4 oz/½ cup bamboo shoots, sliced

Method

1. Bring the stock to the boil in a large saucepan. If the stock is not rich enough, add a stock cube.

2. Add the tofu and simmer for 10 minutes. Then add the remaining ingredients and simmer for a further 10 minutes. Serve hot.

Serves 4

Crab and Scallop Soup

Ingredients

25 g/1 oz dried mushrooms
5 ml/1 tsp vegetable oil
1 egg, beaten
1.5 litres/2 ½ pts/6 cups chicken stock
175 g/6 oz crabmeat, flaked
100 g/4 oz shelled scallops, sliced
100 g/4 oz/½ cup bamboo shoots, sliced
8 spring onions, chopped
2.5 ml/½ tsp grated ginger root
45 ml/3 tbsp cornflour
90 ml/6 tbsp water
30 ml/2 tbsp rice wine or dry sherry
20 ml/4 tsp soy sauce
2 egg whites

Method

1.. Soak the mushrooms in boiling water for 30 minutes. Drain and squeeze out any excess moisture. Remove and discard the stalks. Slice the caps thinly.

2. Heat the oil in a small pan. Add the egg and tilt the pan so that the egg completely covers the bottom. Cook over a medium heat until the egg is set, then turn the omelette over and cook the other side. Remove from the pan, roll up and cut into thin strips.

3. Bring the stock to the boil in a large saucepan. Add the mushrooms, egg strips, crabmeat, scallops, bamboo shoots, spring onions and ginger. Bring back to the boil.

4.   Mix the cornflour with 60 ml/4 tbsp of water, the wine or sherry and the soy sauce. Stir the mixture into the soup and return it to the boil. Beat the egg whites with the remaining water and drizzle this slowly into the soup while stirring vigorously.

Serves 4 to 6

5 | White Turnip Soup

Ingredients

> 1 litre/1 ¾ pts/4 ¼ cups chicken stock
> 1 large turnip, thinly sliced
> 200 g/7 oz lean pork, thinly sliced
> 15 ml/1 tbsp soy sauce
> 60 ml/4 tbsp brandy
> Salt and freshly ground black pepper
> 4 shallots, finely chopped

Method

1.   Bring the stock to the boil in a large saucepan. If the stock is not rich enough, add a stock cube.

2.   Add the turnip and pork and simmer for about 20 minutes until the turnip is tender.

3.   Stir in the soy sauce and brandy, season to taste with salt and pepper and heat through.

4.   Serve sprinkled with the shallots.

Serves 4

Cabbage and Noodle Soup

Ingredients

30 ml/2 tbsp vegetable oil
225 g/8 oz lean pork, cut into thin strips
1.5 litres/2 ½ pts/6 cups chicken stock
30 ml/2 tbsp soy sauce
2.5 ml/½ tsp grated ginger root
100 g/4 oz egg noodles
8 spring onions, diagonally sliced
100 g/4 oz cabbage, shredded

Method

1. Heat the oil in a wok over a medium heat. Stir-fry the pork for about 5 minutes until browned on all sides.

2. Add the stock, soy sauce and ginger, bring to the boil and simmer for 10 minutes.

3. Stir in the noodles, spring onions and cabbage and simmer for about 4 minutes until the noodles are tender.

Serves 4

7 Egg Flower Soup

Ingredients

1 litre/1 ¾ pts/4 ¼ cups clear chicken stock
100 g/4 oz cooked ham, finely chopped
Salt and freshly ground black pepper
2 eggs, beaten
30 ml/2 tbsp chopped shallots

Method

1. Bring the stock to the boil in a large saucepan. If the stock is not rich enough, add a stock cube.

2. Add the ham, season to taste with salt and pepper and simmer for 5 minutes.

3. Slowly pour the beaten eggs through the prongs of a fork into the pan, moving the fork so that the egg covers the surface of the soup. Stir gently to form a flower pattern. Serve sprinkled with chopped shallots.

Serves 4

8 Mongolian Hot Pot

This dish is traditionally served in an oriental fire pot over hot charcoal, but a fondue pot will work equally well. Each diner chooses from the meat and vegetable ingredients offered and cooks them, piece by piece, in the stock. The stock is then served as the final course. Small bowls of accompaniments are offered with the meal, including soy sauce, hoi sin sauce and freshly steamed rice.

Ingredients

For the stock:
1.2 litres/2 pts/5 cups water
1 chicken breast
1 onion, sliced
1 stick celery, sliced
1 chicken stock cube
15 ml/1 tbsp rice wine or dry sherry
2.5 ml/½ tsp sesame oil
2.5 cm/1 in piece ginger root, thinly sliced

For the hot pot:
175 g/6 oz lean beef
175 g/6 oz pork tenderloin
100 g/4 oz chicken livers, thinly sliced
1 chicken breast, cubed
225 g/8 oz fish fillets, cubed
225 g/8 oz peeled prawns
12 oysters, shelled
100 g/4 oz Chinese cabbage, shredded
100 g/4 oz spinach, cut into strips
4 spring onions, sliced
½ cucumber, sliced
100 g/4 oz/½ cup bamboo shoots, sliced
100 g/4 oz tofu, sliced

Method

1. Mix together all the stock ingredients in a large saucepan, cover and bring to the boil then simmer for about 2 hours. Strain.

2. Wrap the beef and pork in freezer wrap and freeze for about 1 hour. Slice the meat across the grain into thin slices.

3. Arrange the meats and other ingredients on serving plates, cover and refrigerate until ready to serve.

4. Bring the stock to the boil then pour it into the fondue pot and keep it hot. Arrange the other ingredients around the pot.

5. To serve, provide the diners with chopsticks, fondue forks or small strainers to hold the food. Place it in the simmering stock until cooked to taste.

Serves 4

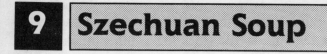

9   Szechuan Soup

Ingredients

25 g/1 oz dried mushrooms
1.5 litres/2 ½ pts/6 cups chicken stock
75 ml/5 tbsp dry white wine
15 ml/1 tbsp soy sauce
2.5 ml/½ tsp chilli sauce
30 ml/2 tbsp cornflour
60 ml/4 tbsp water
100 g/4 oz lean pork, cut into thin strips
75 g/3 oz cooked ham, cut into thin strips
1 small red pepper, seeded and cut into thin strips
75 g/3 oz/⅓ cup water chestnuts, sliced
10 ml/2 tsp white wine vinegar
5 ml/1 tsp sesame oil
1 egg, beaten
175 g/6 oz peeled prawns
6 spring onions, finely chopped
175 g/6 oz tofu, cubed

Method

1.   Soak the mushrooms in boiling water for 30 minutes. Drain and squeeze out any excess moisture. Remove and discard the stems. Slice the caps thinly.

2.   Place the stock in a large saucepan with the wine, soy sauce and chilli sauce. Bring to the boil, cover and simmer for 5 minutes.

3.   Blend the cornflour with 45 ml/3 tbsp of water and mix it into the soup, stirring until the soup boils and thickens. Add the mushrooms, pork, ham, pepper and water chestnuts and simmer, uncovered, for 5 minutes.

4.   Stir in the vinegar and sesame oil. Beat the egg with the remaining water and drizzle this into the soup, stirring vigorously.

5.   Add the prawns, spring onions and tofu and simmer for a few minutes to heat through.

Serves 4

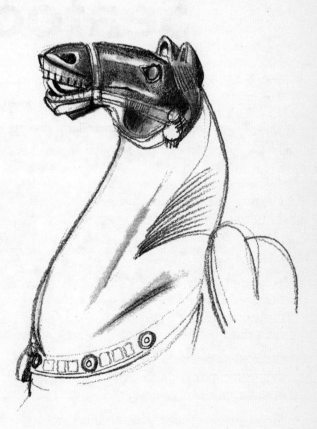

Seafood

Stir-frying and quick cooking are ideal for many seafoods, particularly prawns, which are delicious prepared in the Chinese style.

1 Butterfly Prawns

Ingredients

750 g/1 ½ lb large uncooked prawns
3 egg yolks
10 ml/2 tsp cornflour
2.5 ml/½ tsp salt
A pinch of freshly ground black pepper
2 slices bacon, cut into short strips
450 ml/¾ pt/2 cups vegetable oil

Method

1. Remove the shells and back vein from the prawns, leaving the tails intact. Rinse and pat dry on kitchen paper. Cut a deep slit down the back of each prawn. Flatten the cut side slightly with the fingers.

2. Beat the egg yolks, cornflour, salt and pepper. Dip the prawns into the mixture and place a strip of bacon on the cut side of each prawn.

3. Heat the oil in a wok over a medium heat until very hot. Fry the prawns in batches for about 3 minutes until golden. Remove from the wok and drain on kitchen paper. Serve immediately.

Serves 4

Ingredients

1 egg white
10 ml/2 tsp cornflour
5 ml/1 tsp salt
450 g/1 lb large shelled prawns
250 ml/8 fl oz/1 cup vegetable oil
1 onion, finely chopped
5 ml/1 tsp curry powder
2.5 ml/½ tsp sugar
2.5 ml/½ tsp Chinese chilli powder
60 ml/4 tbsp cream
30 ml/2 tbsp Satay Sauce (page 155)
1 red pepper, seeded and thinly sliced
120 ml/4 fl oz/½ cup brandy (optional)

Method

1. Mix together the egg white, cornflour and salt. Add the prawns, cover and leave to stand for 1 hour.

2. Heat the oil in a wok over a medium heat. Fry the prawns a few at a time for about 1 minute until golden. Remove from the wok and drain on kitchen paper.

3. Remove all but 30 ml/2 tbsp of oil from the wok. Add the onion, curry powder, sugar and chilli powder and stir-fry for 2 minutes. Add the prawns and stir-fry for 1 minute. Add the cream and satay sauce and stir-fry for 1 minute. Mix in the pepper.

4. Arrange the prawn mixture on a serving plate and spoon the sauce over.

5. Heat the brandy, if using, in a small saucepan until just warm and pour it into a small metal bowl near

the serving plate. Carefully ignite the brandy, and hold the prawns in the flame on a long-handled fork for a few seconds before eating.

Serves 4

3 Plaice with Garlic

Ingredients

350 g/12 oz plaice fillets, skinned and cut into strips
Salt
45 ml/3 tbsp cornflour
1 egg, beaten
60 ml/4 tbsp vegetable oil
1 clove garlic, finely chopped
4 spring onions, finely chopped
15 ml/1 tbsp rice wine or dry sherry
5 ml/1 tsp sesame oil

Method

1. Sprinkle the fish with salt and leave to stand for 20 minutes.

2. Dust the fish with cornflour then dip in the egg.

3. Heat the oil in a wok over a medium heat and fry the fish strips a few at a time for about 4 minutes until golden. Remove from the wok and drain on kitchen paper.

4. Drain all but 5 ml/1 tsp of oil from the wok and add the remaining ingredients. Bring to the boil, stirring, and simmer for 3 minutes. Pour over the fish and serve immediately.

Serves 4

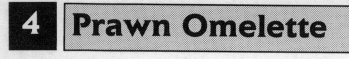 4 Prawn Omelette

Ingredients

250 ml/8 fl oz/1 cup chicken stock
20 ml/4 tsp cornflour
5 ml/1 tsp sugar
10 ml/2 tsp soy sauce
8 eggs
2.5 ml/½ tsp salt
Freshly ground black pepper
45 ml/3 tbsp vegetable oil
100 g/4 oz mushrooms, finely chopped
6 spring onions
225 g/8 oz bean sprouts
225 g/8 oz shelled prawns, finely chopped
1 stick celery, finely chopped

Method

1. Mix together the stock, cornflour, sugar and soy sauce in a saucepan. Bring to the boil, stirring, then simmer for 5 minutes, stirring occasionally. Keep the sauce warm.

2. Beat the eggs, salt and pepper to taste until frothy.

3. Heat 15 ml/1 tbsp of oil in a small frying pan and fry the mushrooms for 1 minute. Stir the mushrooms into the egg mixture.

4. Finely chop 4 of the spring onions and slice the remainder. Mix the chopped spring onions, bean sprouts, prawns and celery into the egg mixture.

5. For each omelette, heat a little oil in an omelette pan. Pour in 120 ml/4 fl oz/½ cup of the egg mixture and cook for about 3 minutes until light brown on each side. Stack the omelettes on serving plates, pour over the warm sauce and serve garnished with sliced spring onions.

Makes 8 omelettes to serve 4

5 Braised Prawns with Vegetables

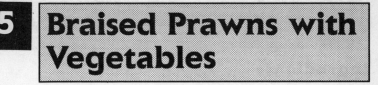

Ingredients

15 ml/1 tbsp vegetable oil
225 g/8 oz broccoli, cut into small florets
225 g/8 oz button mushrooms
225 g/8 oz/1 cup bamboo shoots, sliced
450 g/1 lb large shelled prawns
120 ml/4 fl oz/½ cup chicken stock
5 ml/1 tsp cornflour
5 ml/1 tsp oyster sauce
2.5 ml/½ tsp sugar
2.5 ml/½ tsp grated ginger root
A pinch of freshly ground black pepper

Method

1. Heat the oil in a wok over a high heat. Add the broccoli and stir-fry for 1 minute. Add the mushrooms and bamboo shoots and stir-fry for 2 minutes. Add the prawns and stir-fry for a further 2 minutes.

2. Mix together the remaining ingredients and pour over the prawn mixture. Bring to the boil, stirring, then simmer for a further 1 minute, stirring continuously. Serve immediately.

Serves 4

6 Crab-Stuffed Prawns

Ingredients

For the sauce:
30 ml/2 tbsp vegetable oil
1 small onion, finely chopped
5 ml/1 tsp curry powder
30 ml/2 tbsp rice wine or dry sherry
15 ml/1 tbsp Satay Sauce (page 155)
5 ml/1 tsp sugar
10 ml/2 tsp soy sauce
60 ml/4 tbsp milk or cream

For the prawns:
2 egg whites
20 ml/4 tsp cornflour
15 ml/1 tbsp rice wine or dry sherry
15 ml/1 tbsp soy sauce
2 x 175 g/6 oz cans crabmeat, drained and flaked
8 spring onions, finely chopped
2 sticks celery, finely chopped
750 g/1 ½ lb large uncooked prawns
50 g/2 oz/½ cup plain flour
3 eggs
45 ml/3 tbsp milk
225 g/8 oz/2 cups breadcrumbs
750 ml/1 ¼ pts/3 cups vegetable oil

Method

1.   To make the sauce, heat the oil in a small
       saucepan. Add the onion and cook over a medium
       heat for about 3 minutes until transparent. Add the
       curry powder and cook, stirring, for 1 minute. Add
       the wine or sherry, satay sauce, sugar and soy
       sauce and cook, stirring, for 2 minutes. Blend in

the milk or cream and bring to the boil. Simmer for 2 minutes. Remove from the heat and keep warm.

2. Mix together the egg whites, cornflour, wine or sherry and soy sauce. Mix in the crabmeat, spring onions and celery.

3. Remove the shell and back veins from the prawns, leaving the tails intact. Cut a deep slit into but not through the back of each prawn and flatten them by pounding gently with a mallet or rolling pin. Spoon the crabmeat mixture onto the prawns and press in with the back of a spoon.

4. Dust the prawns lightly with flour. Beat the eggs and milk in a shallow dish. Place each prawn, stuffed side up, in the egg mixture the spoon the mixture over the prawns to cover completely. Coat in breadcrumbs, pressing them lightly on to the prawns. Place the prawns in a single layer on a baking sheet and refrigerate for 30 minutes.

5. Heat the oil in a wok over a medium heat. Fry the prawns in batches for about 3 minutes until golden. Remove from the wok and drain on kitchen paper. Serve hot with the warm sauce.

Serves 4

7 Satay Prawns

Ingredients

20 uncooked king prawns
30 ml/2 tbsp vegetable oil
2 cloves garlic, crushed
5 ml/1 tsp grated ginger root
30 ml/2 tbsp Satay Sauce (page 155)
120 ml/4 fl oz/½ cup chicken stock
5 ml/1 tsp soy sauce
5 ml/1 tsp hoi sin sauce
225 g/8 oz/½ lb bean sprouts

Method

1. Remove and discard the shells and back veins from the prawns, leaving the tails intact.

2. Heat the oil in a wok over a medium heat and fry the garlic and ginger for 1 minute, then remove them from the wok and discard.

3. Add the prawns to the wok and fry for 2 minutes. Add the satay sauce, stock, soy sauce and hoi sin sauce, bring to the boil, cover and simmer for 5 minutes.

4. Meanwhile, blanch the bean sprouts in boiling water for 4 minutes, then drain.

5. Arrange the bean sprouts on a platter and spoon the prawns on top.

Serves 4

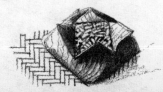

8 Prawn Fries

Ingredients

12 large uncooked prawns
1 egg
30 ml/2 tbsp cornflour
A pinch of salt
A pinch of freshly ground black pepper
3 slices bread
1 hardboiled egg yolk, chopped
25 g/1 oz cooked ham, chopped
1 spring onion, finely chopped
450 ml/¾ pt/2 cups vegetable oil

Method

1. Remove the shells and back veins from the prawns, leaving the tails intact. Cut down the back of the prawns with a sharp knife and gently press them flat with the fingers.

2. Beat the egg, cornflour, salt and pepper. Toss the prawns in the mixture until completely coated.

3. Remove the crusts from the bread and cut it into quarters. Place one prawn, cut side down, on each piece and gently press them down. Brush a little egg mixture over each prawn. Sprinkle with the egg yolk, ham and spring onion.

4. Heat the oil in a wok over a medium heat. Fry the prawn-bread pieces in batches for about 2 minutes until golden. Remove from the wok and drain on kitchen paper. Serve hot.

Makes 12

Scallops with Vegetables

Ingredients

25 g/1 oz dried mushrooms
2 onions
30 ml/2 tbsp vegetable oil
3 sticks celery, diagonally sliced
225 g/8 oz green beans, diagonally sliced
10 ml/2 tsp grated ginger root
1 clove garlic, crushed
20 ml/4 tsp cornflour
250 ml/8 fl oz/1 cup chicken stock
30 ml/2 tbsp rice wine or dry sherry
20 ml/4 tsp soy sauce
450 g/1 lb shelled scallops, quartered
6 spring onions, thinly sliced
1 x 425 g/15 oz can baby corn cobs

Method

1. Soak the mushrooms in boiling water for 30 minutes. Drain and squeeze out any excess moisture. Remove and discard the stalks. Slice the caps thinly. Cut the onions into wedges and separate the layers.

2. Heat the oil in a wok over a high heat. Add the onions, celery, beans, ginger and garlic and stir-fry for 3 minutes.

3. Blend the cornflour with a little of the stock, then mix in the remaining stock, the wine or sherry and the soy sauce. Add to the wok and bring to the boil, stirring.

4. Add the mushrooms, scallops, spring onions and corn and cook, stirring, for about 5 minutes until the scallops are tender.

Serves 4 to 6

10 | Seafood Stir-Fry

Ingredients

60 ml/4 tbsp vegetable oil
8 spring onions, diagonally sliced
3 sticks celery, diagonally sliced
225 g/8 oz/1 cup bamboo shoots, sliced
225 g/8 oz/1 cup water chestnuts, halved
225 g/8 oz shelled scallops
225 g/8 oz shelled prawns
225 g/8 oz cod fillets, skinned and cubed
225 g/8 oz squid, sliced (optional)
120 ml/4 fl oz/½ cup chicken stock
15 ml/1 tbsp soy sauce
10 ml/2 tsp cornflour
10 ml/2 tsp rice wine or dry sherry

Method

1. Heat half the oil in a wok over a high heat. Add the onions, celery, bamboo shoots and water chestnuts and stir-fry for about 2 minutes until crisp-tender. Remove the vegetables from the wok.

2. Heat the remaining oil. Add the scallops, prawns, cod and squid, if using, and stir-fry for about 3 minutes until all the fish is cooked.

3. Mix together the stock, soy sauce, cornflour and wine or sherry. Pour the mixture into the wok and bring to the boil, stirring. Return the vegetables to the wok. Simmer for 2 minutes and serve immediately with fried noodles.

Serves 4 to 6

11 Sweet and Sour Crab Claws

Ingredients

1 quantity Sweet and Sour Sauce (page 154)
100 g/4 oz Chinese Mixed Pickles (page 126),
   drained and sliced
10 thick crab claws
450 g/1 lb uncooked prawns
5 spring onions, finely chopped
2 sticks celery, finely chopped
5 ml/1 tsp grated ginger root
10 ml/2 tsp soy sauce
10 ml/2 tsp oyster sauce
100 g/4 oz/1 cup cornflour
50 g/2 oz/½ cup plain flour
2.5 ml/½ tsp baking powder
2.5 ml/½ tsp salt
150 ml/¼ pt/⅔ cup water
1 litre/1 ¾ pts/4 ¼ cups vegetable oil

Method

1.   Prepare the sweet and sour sauce, stir in the pickles and keep the sauce warm.

2.   Remove the shell from the meat end of each claw using kitchen shears or a crab or nut cracker. If necessary, tap the claw gently with a rolling pin to break the shell. Leave the shell on one part of the pincher for holding the crabmeat.

3.   Remove the shells and back veins from the prawns and chop them finely.

4.   Mix together the prawns, spring onions, celery, ginger, soy sauce and oyster sauce. Divide the

mixture into 8 portions. Flatten one portion in the palm of one hand and place the meat end of a crab claw on top. Carefully press the prawn mixture all round the crabmeat, leaving the shell on the pincher uncovered. Use half the cornflour to coat the crab claws.

5. Mix together the remaining cornflour with the flour, baking powder and salt. Gradually whisk in the water and beat until smooth.

6. Heat the oil in a wok over a high heat. Carefully dip each claw into the batter, coating it completely. Fry the claws a few at a time for about 5 minutes until cooked through and golden. Remove from the wok and drain on kitchen paper. Serve with the sweet and sour sauce.

Serves 5

12 Fried Fish with Lemon Sauce

Ingredients

For the sauce:
450 ml/³⁄₄ pt/2 cups chicken stock
1 x 5 cm/2 in square piece of lemon rind
150 ml/¹⁄₄ pt/²⁄₃ cup lemon juice
90 ml/6 tbsp brown sugar
5 cm/2 in piece ginger root, thinly sliced
45 ml/3 tbsp cornflour

For the fish:
4 x 350 g/12 oz fish, scaled
375 g/12 oz plain flour
175 ml/6 fl oz/³⁄₄ cup water
750 ml/1 ¹⁄₄ pts/3 cups vegetable oil
2 egg whites
8 spring onions, thinly sliced

Method

1. To make the sauce, mix together the stock, lemon rind and juice, sugar and ginger in a saucepan. Bring to the boil then simmer for 5 minutes. Remove from the heat, strain and return to the pan.

2. Mix the cornflour with a little of the stock then stir it into the pan. Bring to the boil, stirring, then simmer for 5 minutes, stirring frequently. Remove the sauce from the heat and keep it warm.

3. Lightly coat the fish on both sides with a little of the flour. Beat the remaining flour with the water

and 10 ml/2 tsp of oil until smooth. Beat the egg whites until stiff but not dry and fold them into the batter.

4.   Heat the remaining oil in a wok over a high heat. Dip the fish in the batter, turning to coat it completely. Cook the fish in the oil, in batches if necessary, for about 10 minutes, turning once, until cooked through and golden. Remove from the wok and drain on kitchen paper.

5.   Arrange the fish on a serving platter. Stir the spring onions into the warm sauce, pour over the fish and serve immediately.

Serves 4

13 Ginger-Spiced Fish

Ingredients

For the sauce:
1 x 225 g/8 oz can tomato purée
30 ml/2 tbsp rice wine or dry sherry
15 ml/1 tbsp grated ginger root
15 ml/1 tbsp Chinese chilli sauce
15 ml/1 tbsp water
15 ml/1 tbsp soy sauce
10 ml/2 tsp sugar
3 cloves garlic, crushed

For the fish:
100 g/4 oz/1 cup plain flour
75 ml/5 tbsp cornflour
175 ml/6 fl oz/¾ cup water
1 egg white
2.5 ml/½ tsp salt
750 ml/1 ¼ pts/3 cups vegetable oil
450 g/1 lb cod fillets, skinned and cubed

Method

1. To make the sauce, combine all the sauce ingredients in a small saucepan and bring to the boil over a medium heat. Cook, stirring, for 2 minutes then remove from the heat.

2. Beat together the flour, cornflour, water, egg white and salt until smooth.

3. Heat the oil in a wok over a high heat. Dip the fish pieces in the batter. Fry a few at a time for about 5 minutes until cooked through and golden. Remove from the wok and drain on kitchen paper.

4. Remove the oil from the wok. Place the fish and sauce in the wok and cook over a medium heat for about 3 minutes, tossing lightly, until the fish is hot throughout and completely coated in the sauce.

Serves 4

14 Chinese Fish Cakes

Ingredients

450 g/1 lb minced cod
5 ml/1 tsp salt
5 ml/1 tsp sugar
45 ml/3 tsp vegetable oil
15 ml/1 tbsp cornflour

Method

1. Mix together the cod, salt, sugar and 10 ml/2 tsp of vegetable oil. Knead together thoroughly, sprinkling with a little cornflour from time to time, until the mixture is soft and elastic. Shape into 4 fish cakes.

2. Heat the remaining oil in a wok over a medium heat and fry the fish cakes for about 10 minutes until golden, pressing them flat as they cook. Serve hot or cold.

Serves 4

Poultry

General Notes

Chicken and duck are very popular in Chinese cooking and there are a wealth of recipes to savour, many of them wonderfully simple to prepare.

Recipes for Chinese chicken often use pieces that are smaller than a standard chicken portion, but it is simple to cut a chicken into suitable pieces. A cleaver is the best utensil to use, but a sharp knife or kitchen shears can be used.

Place the chicken, breast side up, on a heavy cutting board. Cut the chicken in half lengthways, cutting slightly to one side of the breast bone and back bone. Remove and discard the back bone. Pull each leg up slightly from the breast section. Cut through the ball and socket joint to remove each leg. Cut through the knee joint of each leg to separate into a drumstick and thigh. Pull each wing away from the breast and cut through the joint next to the breast. Cut each drumstick, thigh and breast piece crosswise into three pieces, cutting completely through the bones. Cut each wing into two pieces to give 22 small serving-sized pieces.

1 | Chicken and Cashew Nuts

Ingredients

225 g/8 oz chicken breasts
1 egg white
5 ml/1 tsp salt
5 ml/1 tsp cornflour
175 ml/6 fl oz/¾ cup vegetable oil
50 g/2 oz cashew nuts
15 ml/1 tbsp soy sauce
15 ml/1 tbsp rice wine or dry sherry
4 Spring Onion Curls (page 11)

Method

1. Remove and discard the skin and bones from the chicken. Cut the chicken into cubes.

2. Mix together the chicken, egg white, salt and cornflour and refrigerate for 30 minutes.

3. Heat the oil in a wok over a medium heat. Add the chicken mixture and stir-fry for 4 minutes until the chicken is cooked through. Remove the chicken from the pan and drain on kitchen paper.

4. Remove all but 15 ml/1 tbsp of oil from the wok and reheat the oil. Add the cashew nuts and stir-fry for 2 minutes. Add the soy sauce, wine or sherry and chicken and stir-fry for 3 minutes. Serve garnished with the spring onion curls.

Serves 4

2 | Chicken Chow Mein

Ingredients

1 quantity Fried Noodles (page 135)
2 chicken breasts
225 g/8 oz lean pork
30 ml/2 tbsp rice wine or dry sherry
30 ml/2 tbsp soy sauce
15 ml/1 tbsp cornflour
30 ml/2 tbsp vegetable oil
1 clove garlic, crushed
2.5 cm/1 in piece ginger root, finely chopped
2 onions, chopped
1 red or green pepper, seeded and sliced
2 sticks celery, diagonally sliced
8 spring onions, chopped
100 g/4 oz white cabbage, shredded
225 g/8 oz shelled prawns
120 ml/4 fl oz/½ cup chicken stock

Method

1.   Prepare the fried noodles.

2.   Remove and discard the skin and bones from the
      chicken. Cut the chicken and pork into 2.5 cm/1 in
      pieces. Blend 10 ml/2 tsp each of the wine or
      sherry and soy sauce with 5 ml/1 tsp of the
      cornflour. Mix in the chicken and pork, cover and
      leave to stand for 1 hour.

3.   Heat the oil in a wok over a high heat. Add the
      garlic and ginger and stir-fry for 1 minute. Add the
      chicken and pork and stir-fry for about 5 minutes
      until the pork is no longer pink. Add the onions,
      pepper, celery, spring onions and cabbage and stir-
      fry for about 5 minutes until the vegetables are
      crisp-tender. Add the prawns.

4.   Mix together the remaining wine or sherry, soy sauce, cornflour and stock. Pour into the wok, bring to the boil and simmer, stirring for about 1 minute until thick.

5.   Arrange the noodles on a serving plate, spoon over the chow mein and serve immediately.

Serves 4 to 6

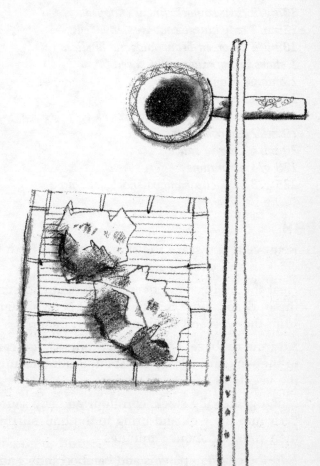

3 | Chicken and Pork Chop Suey

Ingredients

2 cooked chicken breasts
45 ml/3 tbsp vegetable oil
225 g/8 oz lean pork, finely chopped
225 g/8 oz Chinese cabbage, shredded
100 g/4 oz green beans, diagonally sliced
3 sticks celery, diagonally sliced
2 onions, chopped
1 large carrot, finely chopped
250 ml/8 fl oz/1 cup chicken stock
10 ml/2 tsp cornflour
20 ml/4 tsp soy sauce
225 g/8 oz prawns
225 g/8 oz/1 cup bamboo shoots, sliced

Method

1. Remove and discard the skin and bones from the chicken and chop coarsely.

2. Heat the oil in a wok over a high heat and stir-fry the pork for about 5 minutes until brown. Remove from the wok and drain on kitchen paper.

3. Add the cabbage, beans, celery, onions and carrot to the wok and stir-fry for about 3 minutes until the vegetables are crisp-tender.

4. Mix together the stock, cornflour and soy sauce. Pour into the wok and bring to the boil, stirring, then cook for about 3 minutes.

5. Add the chicken, prawns and bamboo shoots and stir-fry for a further 3 minutes until heated through.

Serves 4 to 6

4 Honey Spiced Chicken

Ingredients

1 x 1.5 kg/3 lb chicken
50 g/2 oz/½ cup plain flour
2.5 ml/½ tsp salt
750 ml/1¼ pts/3 cups vegetable oil
10 ml/2 tsp grated ginger root
45 ml/3 tbsp honey
75 ml/5 tbsp water
75 ml/5 tbsp lemon juice
10 ml/2 tsp cornflour
20 ml/4 tsp chilli sauce
10 ml/2 tsp soy sauce
6 spring onions, cut into thin lengthways slices

Method

1. Remove the giblets from the chicken and cut into serving-sized pieces (see page 64).

2. Mix together the flour and salt and coat the chicken pieces in the flour.

3. Heat the oil in a wok over a high heat. Fry the chicken pieces a few at a time for about 5 minutes until golden. Drain on kitchen paper.

3. Pour all but 15 ml/1 tbsp of the oil out of the wok. Add the ginger and stir-fry for 1 minute. Add the honey and stir-fry for 1 minute.

4. Mix together the water, lemon juice, cornflour, chilli sauce and soy sauce. Add this to the wok and bring to the boil, stirring continuously.

5. Add the chicken pieces to the wok and cook for about 10 minutes, stirring, until the chicken is cooked through. Stir in the spring onions and cook for a further 1 minute.

Serves 4 to 6

5 Almond Chicken

Ingredients

375 ml/13 fl oz/1 ½ cups water
60 ml/4 tbsp rice wine or dry sherry
45 ml/3 tbsp cornflour
20 ml/4 tsp soy sauce
5 ml/1 tsp chicken stock granules
4 chicken breasts
1 egg white
2.5 ml/½ tsp salt
750 ml/1 ¼ pts/3 cups vegetable oil
75 g/3 oz/½ cup blanched almonds
1 large carrot, diced
5 ml/1 tsp grated ginger root
6 spring onions, cut into 2.5 cm/1 in pieces
3 sticks celery, diagonally sliced
100 g/4 oz mushrooms, sliced
100 g/4 oz/½ cup bamboo shoots, sliced

Method

1. Mix together the water, 30 ml/2 tbsp of the wine or sherry, 30 ml/2 tbsp of cornflour, the soy sauce and stock granules in a small saucepan. Bring to the boil, stirring, and simmer for about 5 minutes until the mixture thickens. Remove from the heat and keep warm.

2. Remove the skin and bones from the chicken and cut it into 2.5 cm/1 in pieces. Mix together the remaining wine or sherry and cornflour, the egg white and salt. Add the chicken pieces.

3. Heat the oil in a wok over a high heat until very hot. Fry the chicken pieces a few at a time for about 5 minutes until light brown. Remove from the wok and drain on kitchen paper.

4.	Remove all but 30 ml/2 tbsp of oil from the wok and stir-fry the almonds for 2 minutes until golden. Remove from the wok and drain on kitchen paper.

5.	Add the carrot and ginger and stir-fry for 1 minute. Add the remaining vegetables and stir-fry for about 3 minutes until the vegetables are crisp-tender. Return the chicken and almonds to the wok with the sauce and stir-fry for a few minutes until hot.

Serves 4 to 6

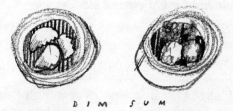

DIM SUM

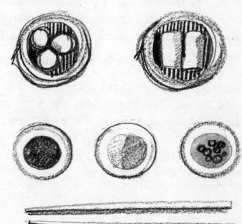

Chicken with Peppers

Ingredients

450 g/1 lb chicken meat, cubed
60 ml/4 tbsp cornflour
750 ml/1 ¼ pts/3 cups vegetable oil
450 g/1 lb onions, chopped
1 small cucumber, diced
1 green pepper, seeded and diced
1 red pepper, seeded and diced
150 ml/¼ pt/⅔ cup chicken stock
Salt and freshly ground black pepper

Method

1. Toss the chicken in half the cornflour.

2. Heat the oil in a wok over a high heat until very hot. Fry the chicken pieces a few at a time for about 5 minutes until cooked through and golden. Remove from the wok and drain on kitchen paper.

3. Toss the vegetables in the remaining cornflour.

4. Remove all but 45 ml/3 tbsp of oil from the wok and stir-fry the vegetables for 5 minutes until lightly browned. Return the chicken to the wok and add the stock. Bring to the boil, stirring, and season to taste with salt and pepper. Simmer for 5 minutes before serving.

Serves 4

7 | Chicken and Lychees

Ingredients

3 chicken breasts
60 ml/4 tbsp cornflour
45 ml/3 tbsp vegetable oil
6 spring onions, cut into 2.5 cm/1 in pieces
1 red pepper, seeded and cut into 2.5 cm/1 in pieces
120 ml/4 fl oz/½ cup tomato sauce
120 ml/4 fl oz/½ cup chicken stock
5 ml/1 tsp sugar
275 g/10 oz peeled lychees
Vermicelli (page 133)

Method

1. Cut the chicken breasts in half and remove and discard the bones. Cut each breast half into 6.

2. Reserve 5 ml/1 tsp of cornflour and toss the chicken in the remainder until it is well coated.

3. Heat the oil in a wok over a high heat and stir-fry the chicken for about 8 minutes until golden brown. Add the onions and pepper and stir-fry for 1 minute.

4. Mix together the tomato sauce, half the stock and the sugar and mix it into the wok with the lychees. Bring to the boil, cover and simmer for about 10 minutes until the chicken is cooked through.

5. Mix the reserved cornflour into the reserved stock and stir it into the chicken. Cook, stirring, until the mixture boils and thickens. Serve with vermicelli.

Serves 4

8 Lemon Chicken

Ingredients

4 chicken breasts
50 g/2 oz/½ cup cornflour
2.5 ml/½ tsp salt
A pinch of freshly ground black pepper
60 ml/4 tbsp water
4 egg yolks, lightly beaten
750 ml/1 ¼ pts/3 cups vegetable oil
4 spring onions, sliced

For the lemon sauce:
375 ml/13 fl oz/1 ½ cups chicken stock
120 ml/4 fl oz/½ cup lemon juice
50 g/2 oz/¼ cup light brown sugar
45 ml/3 tbsp cornflour
45 ml/3 tbsp honey
5 ml/1 tsp grated ginger root

Method

1. Remove the skin from the chicken and discard. Cut the breasts in half and remove and discard the bones. Pound the chicken breasts lightly with a mallet or rolling pin.

2. Mix together the cornflour, salt and pepper and gradually blend in the water and egg yolks.

3. Heat the oil in a wok over a high heat. Dip the chicken into the egg mixture then fry for about 5 minutes in the hot oil until golden. Drain on kitchen paper.

4. Meanwhile, combine all the sauce ingredients in a saucepan and bring to the boil, stirring continuously, then simmer for 5 minutes.

5. Cut each breast into 3 or 4 pieces and arrange on a serving plate. Pour over the sauce and serve garnished with the spring onions.

Serves 4 to 6

Chicken with Water Chestnuts

Ingredients

25 g/1 oz dried mushrooms
2 chicken breasts
1 onion
375 ml/13 fl oz/1 ½ cups vegetable oil
3 sticks celery, sliced
1 red or green pepper, seeded and sliced
225 g/8 oz/1 cup water chestnuts, halved
225 g/8 oz/½ lb bean sprouts
2.5 cm/1 in piece ginger root, thinly sliced
160 ml/¼ pt/⅔ cup chicken stock
20 ml/4 tsp cornflour
15 ml/1 tbsp rice wine or dry sherry
15 ml/1 tbsp soy sauce
15 ml/1 tbsp oyster sauce

Method

1. Soak the mushrooms in boiling water for 30 minutes. Drain and squeeze out any excess moisture. Remove and discard the stems. Cut the caps into halves.

2. Remove and discard the skin and bones from the chicken. Cut the chicken into 2.5 cm/1 in pieces. Cut the onion into wedges and separate the layers.

3. Heat the oil in a wok over a high heat and stir-fry the chicken for 5 minutes until golden. Remove from the wok and drain on kitchen paper.

4. Remove all but 30 ml/2 tbsp of oil from the wok. Heat the oil and stir-fry the celery, pepper, onion, water chestnuts, bean sprouts, ginger and chicken, stirring to combine them.

5.   Mix together the stock, cornflour, wine or sherry, soy sauce and oyster sauce and pour it over the chicken. Bring to the boil and cook, stirring, for about 5 minutes until the vegetables are crisp-tender.

Serves 4

10 Chicken with Mangoes

Ingredients

100 g/4 oz/1 cup plain flour
400 ml/14 fl oz/1 ¾ cups water
2.5 ml/½ tsp salt
A pinch of baking powder
3 chicken breasts
750 ml/1 ¼ pts/3 cups vegetable oil
2.5 cm/1 in piece ginger root, thinly sliced
45 ml/3 tbsp white wine vinegar
45 ml/3 tbsp rice wine or dry sherry
20 ml/4 tsp soy sauce
10 ml/2 tsp sugar
10 ml/2 tsp cornflour
10 ml/2 tsp chicken stock granules
5 ml/1 tsp sesame oil
8 spring onions, cut into 1 cm/½ in pieces
1 x 400 g/11 oz can mangoes, drained and cut into
strips

Method

1. Whisk together the flour, 250 ml/8 fl oz/1 cup of
    water, the salt and baking powder. Leave to stand
    for 15 minutes.

2. Remove and discard the skin and bones from the
    chicken. Cut into thin strips. Mix these into the
    flour mixture.

3. Heat the oil in a wok over a high heat until very
    hot. Fry the chicken strips a few at a time for
    about 5 minutes until golden. Remove and drain
    on kitchen paper.

4. Remove all but 15 ml/1 tbsp of oil from the wok. Reduce the heat to medium, add the ginger and stir-fry for about 2 minutes until light brown.

5. Mix together the remaining water with the wine vinegar, wine or sherry, soy sauce, sugar, cornflour, stock granules and sesame oil. Increase the heat, add to the wok and bring to the boil, stirring. Add the spring onions, reduce the heat again and simmer for 3 minutes.

6. Add the chicken and mangoes and stir-fry for 2 minutes. Serve immediately.

Serves 4 to 6

Regional Styles

11 Chicken with Hoi Sin Sauce

Ingredients

1 x 1.5 kg/3 lb chicken
50 g/2 oz cornflour
750 ml/1 ¼ pts/3 cups vegetable oil
10 ml/2 tsp grated ginger root
2 onions, chopped
225 g/8 oz broccoli, cut into small florets
1 red or green pepper, seeded and chopped
225 g/8 oz button mushrooms
250 ml/8 fl oz/1 cup chicken stock
45 ml/3 tbsp rice wine or dry sherry
45 ml/3 tbsp cider vinegar
45 ml/3 tbsp hoi sin sauce
20 ml/4 tsp soy sauce

Method

1. Cut the chicken into serving-size pieces (see page 64). Coat with half the cornflour.

2. Heat the oil in a wok over a high heat. Fry the chicken pieces a few at a time for about 8 minutes until golden and cooked through. Remove from the work and drain on kitchen paper.

3. Remove all but 30 ml/2 tbsp of oil from the wok and stir-fry the ginger over a medium heat for 1 minute. Add the onions and stir-fry for 1 minute. Add the broccoli, pepper and mushrooms and stir-fry for 2 minutes.

4.　　Combine the stock with all the remaining ingredients and add to the wok. Bring to the boil, stirring, and cook until the sauce becomes translucent.

5.　　Return the chicken to the wok and cook, stirring, for about 2 minutes until heated through.

Serves 4 to 6

12 Five-Spice Chicken

Ingredients

2 x 1.5 kg/3 lb chickens
250 ml/8 fl oz/1 cup soy sauce
2.5 cm/1 in piece ginger root, shredded
2 cloves garlic, crushed
15 ml/1 tbsp five-spice powder
45 ml/3 tbsp rice wine or dry sherry
45 ml/3 tbsp honey
2.5 ml/½ tsp sesame oil
750 ml/1¼ pts/3 cups vegetable oil
60 ml/4 tbsp salt
2.5 ml/½ tsp freshly ground black pepper

Method

1. Remove the giblets from the chickens and reserve for another use. Place the chickens in a large saucepan and add enough water to cover. Reserve 15 ml/1 tbsp of the soy sauce and add the remainder to the chickens with the ginger, garlic and 10 ml/2 tsp of five-spice powder. Bring to the boil, cover and simmer for 5 minutes. Turn off the heat and leave the chickens to stand in the water until the water is lukewarm. Drain the chickens.

2. Cut the chickens in half lengthways through the breast bone and along the back bone. Place cut-side down in baking tins.

3. Mix together the wine or sherry, honey, sesame oil, remaining soy sauce and five-spice powder. Rub the mixture over the chickens and leave to stand for 2 hours, brushing occasionally with the mixture.

4. Heat the oil in a wok over a high heat until very hot. Cook half a chicken at a time for 10 minutes until browned and cooked through. Drain on kitchen paper and cut into serving-sized pieces (see page 64).

5. Meanwhile, mix the salt and pepper in a dry frying pan and fry over a medium heat for 2 minutes. Stir in the remaining five-spice powder and cook for a further 1 minute. Divide between small dishes and serve as a dip for the chicken.

Serves 6

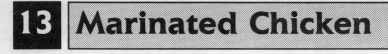 **13 Marinated Chicken**

Ingredients

45 ml/3 tbsp soy sauce
45 ml/3 tbsp rice wine or dry sherry
30 ml/2 tbsp light brown sugar
5 ml/1 tsp grated ginger root
2 cloves garlic, crushed
6 spring onions, diagonally sliced
750 g/1 ½ lb chicken wings
30 ml/2 tbsp vegetable oil
225 g/8 oz/1 cup bamboo shoots, sliced
20 ml/4 tsp cornflour
175 ml/6 fl oz/¾ cup chicken stock

- Method

1. Mix together the soy sauce, wine or sherry, sugar, ginger, garlic and onions. Add the chicken wings and toss to coat completely. Cover and leave to stand for 1 hour, stirring occasionally.

2. Heat the oil in a wok over a high heat and stir-fry the bamboo shoots for 2 minutes. Remove them from the wok.

3. Drain the chicken and onions, reserving the marinade. Reheat the wok and stir-fry the chicken and onions for about 5 minutes until the chicken is browned on all sides. Reduce the heat to low and cook for a further 20 minutes until the chicken is tender.

4. Blend the cornflour with the stock and reserved marinade. Pour the mixture over the chicken and bring to the boil, stirring until the mixture thickens. Stir in the bamboo shoots and stir-fry for a further 2 minutes.

Serves 4

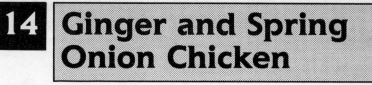

14 | Ginger and Spring Onion Chicken

Ingredients

1 x 1.5 kg/3 lb chicken
5 cm/2 in piece ginger root
Salt and freshly ground black pepper
90 ml/6 tbsp vegetable oil
8 spring onions, finely chopped
10 ml/2 tsp white wine vinegar
5 ml/1 tsp soy sauce
1 quantity Steamed Rice (page 128)

Method

1. Place the chicken in a large saucepan or flameproof casserole. Slice half the ginger and add it to the pan with enough water almost to cover the chicken. Season to taste with salt and pepper. Cover, bring to the boil and simmer for about 1 hour until tender. Leave the chicken to stand in the stock until cool.

2. Drain the chicken and refrigerate until cold. Cut into serving pieces (see page 64).

3. Grate the remaining ginger. Combine the ginger, oil, onions, wine vinegar and soy sauce in a screwtop jar and season to taste with salt and pepper. Cover and shake well, then refrigerate for 1 to 2 hours.

4. Place the chicken pieces in a serving bowl and dress with the ginger dressing. Serve with steamed rice.

Serves 4 to 6

15 Chicken and Pineapple

Ingredients

1 x 1.5 kg/3 lb chicken
50 g/2 oz/½ cup cornflour
750 ml/1 ¼ pts/3 cups vegetable oil
10 ml/2 tsp grated ginger root
1 clove garlic, crushed
1 x 500 g/1 lb 2 oz can pineapple chunks, drained
1 red or green pepper, seeded and thinly sliced
375 ml/13 fl oz/1 ½ cups chicken stock
30 ml/2 tbsp honey
15 ml/1 tbsp sesame oil
4 spring onions, thinly sliced

Method

1. Cut the chicken into serving-size pieces (see page 64). Reserve 10 ml/2 tsp of cornflour and use the rest to coat the chicken pieces.

2. Heat the oil in a wok over a high heat. Fry the chicken pieces a few at a time for about 8 minutes until golden and cooked through. Remove from the wok and drain on kitchen paper.

3. Remove all but 30 ml/2 tbsp of the oil from the wok, add the ginger and garlic and stir-fry for 1 minute over a medium heat. Add the pineapple and pepper and stir-fry over a high heat for 2 minutes. Remove the mixture from the wok.

4. Mix the stock with the reserved cornflour and blend in the honey and sesame oil. Pour into the wok, bring to the boil and cook for 3 minutes, stirring, until the sauce is thick.

5. Return the chicken and vegetables to the wok and cook, stirring, until heated through. Add the spring onions and cook for a further 1 minute, then serve immediately.

Serves 4

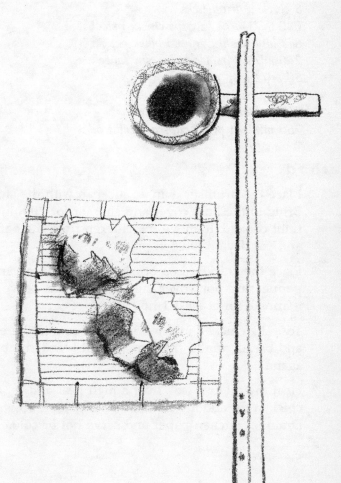

16 | Hoi Sin Chicken Drumsticks

Ingredients

8 chicken drumsticks
600 ml/1 pt/2 ½ cups chicken stock
Salt and freshly ground black pepper
250 ml/8 fl oz/1 cup hoi sin sauce
30 ml/2 tbsp plain flour
2 eggs, beaten
100 g/4 oz/1 cup breadcrumbs
750 ml/1 ¼ pts/3 cups vegetable oil

Method

1.   Place the drumsticks in a saucepan with the stock. Bring to the boil, cover and simmer for 20 minutes until cooked. Remove the chicken from the pan and pat dry on kitchen paper.

2.   Place the chicken in a bowl, season with salt and pepper and pour over the hoi sin sauce. Leave to marinate for at least 1 hour.

3.   Toss the chicken in the flour, then coat in the eggs and breadcrumbs, then in egg and breadcrumbs again.

4.   Heat the oil in a wok over a high heat and fry the chicken for about 5 minutes until golden brown. Drain on kitchen paper and serve hot or cold.

Serves 4

17 Sesame Chicken Salad

Ingredients

15 ml/1 tbsp sesame seeds
3 chicken breasts
1.5 litres/2 ½ pts/6 cups water
30 ml/2 tbsp soy sauce
2.5 ml/½ tsp salt
2.5 ml/½ tsp five-spice powder
3 sticks celery, diagonally sliced
15 ml/1 tbsp sesame oil
15 ml/1 tbsp vegetable oil
A pinch of ground ginger
A pinch of freshly ground black pepper

Method

1. Sprinkle the sesame seeds into a small, shallow baking tin and bake in a preheated oven at 180°C/ 350°F for about 5 minutes until golden.

2. Place the chicken, water, 15 ml/1 tbsp of soy sauce, the salt and five-spice powder in a large saucepan. Bring to the boil, cover and simmer for 20 minutes. Remove from the heat and leave the chicken to stand in the water for 1 hour.

3. Remove the chicken, reserving the stock, and drain. Remove and discard the bones and cut the meat into thick slices.

4. Bring the stock back to the boil, add the celery and cook for about 2 minutes until crisp-tender. Drain well.

5. Mix together the remaining soy sauce with the oils, ginger and pepper and add the chicken and celery. Toss well, transfer to a serving dish and serve sprinkled with sesame seeds.

Serves 4

18 | Slow-Cook Duck

Ingredients

1 x 1.75 kg/4 lb duck
50 g/2 oz cornflour
750 ml/1 ¼ pts/3 cups vegetable oil
2 cloves garlic, crushed
30 ml/2 tbsp rice wine or dry sherry
30 ml/2 tbsp soy sauce
5 ml/1 tsp grated ginger root
750 ml/1 ¼ pts/3 cups chicken stock
25 g/1 oz dried mushrooms
225 g/8 oz/1 cup bamboo shoots, sliced
225 g/8 oz/1 cup water chestnuts, sliced
10 ml/2 tsp sugar
A pinch of freshly ground black pepper
5 spring onions, sliced

Method

1. Cut the duck into serving-sized pieces (see page 64). Reserve 30 ml/2 tbsp of cornflour and coat the duck in the remainder.

2. Heat the oil in a wok over a high heat until very hot. Add the garlic and fry the duck a few pieces at a time for about 5 minutes until brown. Remove the duck from the wok and drain on kitchen paper.

3. Place the duck in a large saucepan. Mix together the wine or sherry, 15 ml/1 tbsp of soy sauce and the ginger. Add to the pan and cook over a high heat for 2 minutes. Add 450 ml/¾ pt/2 cups of stock and bring to the boil. Cover and simmer over a low heat for about 1 hour until the duck is tender.

4.   Meanwhile soak the mushrooms in boiling water for 30 minutes. Drain and squeeze out any excess moisture. Remove and discard the stems. Slice the caps thinly.

5.   Add the mushrooms, bamboo shoots and water chestnuts to the pan and cook, stirring frequently, for 5 minutes. Skim off any fat from the liquid.

6.   Blend the remaining stock, cornflour and soy sauce with the sugar and pepper. Stir into the pan and bring to the boil, stirring. Simmer for about 5 minutes until the sauce thickens.

7.   Transfer to a warmed serving bowl and serve garnished with spring onion slices.

Serves 4 to 6

19 Pineapple Duck

Ingredients

1 x 1.75 kg/4 lb duck
300 ml/½ pt/1 ¼ cups water
90 ml/6 tbsp rice wine or dry sherry
60 ml/4 tbsp white wine vinegar
60 ml/4 tbsp soy sauce
60 ml/4 tbsp barbecue sauce
A pinch of five-spice powder
1 small ripe pineapple
30 ml/2 tbsp vegetable oil
10 ml/2 tsp grated ginger root
1 clove garlic, crushed
15 ml/1 tbsp cornflour
4 spring onions, diagonally sliced
Spring Onion Curls (page 11)

Method

1. Place the duck on a rack in a baking tin. Mix together 120 ml/4 fl oz/½ cup of water with 45 ml/3 tbsp each of the wine or sherry, wine vinegar, soy sauce and barbecue sauce. Add the five-spice powder. Pour the mixture over the duck and roast in a preheated oven at 220°C/425°F/gas mark 7 for about 20 minutes until light brown, basting frequently.

2. Reduce the heat to 180°C/350°F/gas mark 4 and roast for a further 1 hour, basting and turning frequently. Remove the duck from the oven and leave to cool completely.

3. Cut the duck in half and remove and discard the backbone. Cut into small serving-size pieces (see page 64).

4.   Remove the top leaves and skin from the pineapple. Cut it into quarters, cut out and discard the core. Slice the pineapple quarters.

5.   Heat the oil in a wok over a high heat. Add the ginger and garlic and stir-fry for 1 minute. Add the duck and stir-fry for 3 minutes. Mix together the remaining water, wine or sherry, wine vinegar, soy sauce, barbecue sauce and the cornflour. Add this to the wok and bring to the boil, stirring. Cook for 3 minutes. Add the pineapple and spring onions and cook for a further 2 minutes until heated through. Serve garnished with spring onion curls.

Serves 4 to 6

20 | Peking Duck

Ingredients

1 x 1.8 kg/4 lb duck
900 ml/1 ½ pts/3 ¾ cups water
1 lemon, thinly sliced
45 ml/3 tbsp soy sauce
45 ml/3 tbsp honey
45 ml/3 tbsp rice wine or dry sherry
1 quantity Chinese Pancakes (page 137)
8 Spring Onion Curls (page 11)
Hoi sin sauce

Method

1. Clean the duck and pat it dry on kitchen paper.

2. Mix together the water, lemon, soy sauce, honey and wine or sherry in a saucepan. Bring to the boil then simmer for 30 minutes.

3. Stand the duck on a rack over a roasting tin and pour the sauce over the duck, turning to coat all sides. Leave to stand for at least 4 hours to dry.

4. Roast the duck in a preheated oven at 240°C/ 475°F/gas mark 9 for 15 minutes. Reduce the heat to 180°C/350°F/gas mark 4 and roast for a further 1½ hours until the duck is tender.

5. Remove the duck from the oven, leave to stand for 15 minutes then carve the skin and meat into small pieces. Serve with pancakes, spring onion curls and hoi sin sauce.

Serves 4

Meat

This selection of meat dishes includes stir-fried dishes and braised dishes which give an idea of the range of Chinese foods. The recipes rely on the best quality ingredients, freshly prepared and cooked.

1 Beef Chow Mein

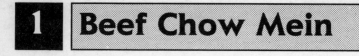

Ingredients

750 g/1 ½ lb rump steak
2 onions
45 ml/3 tbsp soy sauce
45 ml/3 tbsp rice wine or dry sherry
15 ml/1 tbsp Satay Sauce (page 155)
350 g/12 oz egg noodles
60 ml/4 tbsp vegetable oil
175 ml/6 fl oz/¾ cup chicken stock
15 ml/1 tbsp cornflour
30 ml/2 tbsp oyster sauce
3 sticks celery, diagonally sliced
100 g/4 oz mushrooms, sliced
1 red or green pepper, seeded and cut into strips
100 g/4 oz/¼ lb bean sprouts, rinsed and drained

Method

1.   Remove and discard the fat from the meat. Cut the meat across the grain into thin slices. Cut the onions into wedges and separate the layers.

2.   Mix together 15 ml/1 tbsp of soy sauce with 15 ml/1 tbsp of the wine or sherry and the satay sauce. Stir in the meat, cover and leave to stand for 1 hour.

3.   Cook the noodles until tender according to the instructions on the packet. Drain well.

4.   Heat 15 ml/1 tbsp of oil in a wok over medium heat. Add the noodles and 15 ml/1 tbsp of soy sauce and stir-fry for 2 minutes until the noodles are light brown. Transfer the noodles to a serving plate and keep them warm.

5. Mix together the stock, cornflour, oyster sauce, remaining wine or sherry and remaining soy sauce.

6. Heat 15 ml/1 tbsp of oil in the wok over a high heat and stir-fry the onions for 1 minute. Add the celery, mushrooms, pepper and bean sprouts and stir-fry for 2 minutes. Remove the vegetables from the wok.

7. Heat the remaining oil in the wok over a high heat. Add the meat and stir-fry for about 5 minutes until the meat is browned. Add the stock mixture, bring to the boil, cover and cook for 3 minutes.

8. Return the vegetables to the wok and cook, stirring, for about 3 minutes until hot. Spoon the mixture over the noodles and serve.

Serves 4

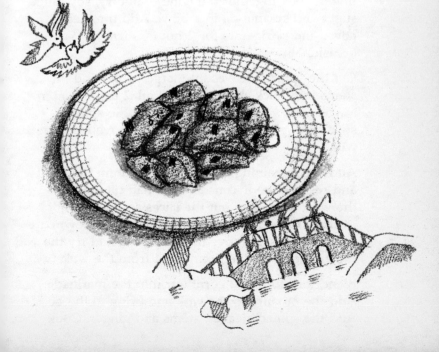

2 | Marinated Beef

Ingredients

450 g/1 lb lean beef, thinly sliced
45 ml/3 tbsp rice wine or dry sherry
15 ml/1 tbsp soy sauce
5 ml/1 tsp sugar
2.5 ml/½ tsp sesame oil
450 g/1 lb spinach
45 ml/3 tbsp vegetable oil
5 cm/2 in piece ginger root, thinly sliced
30 ml/2 tbsp beef stock
2.5 ml/½ tsp cornflour

Method

1. Flatten the meat slightly by pressing with the fingers. Mix together the wine or sherry, soy sauce, sugar and sesame oil in a bowl. Add the meat, cover and refrigerate for 2 hours, stirring occasionally.

2. Cut the spinach leaves into large pieces and the stems into thick slices. Heat 30 ml/2 tbsp of oil in a wok over a high heat and stir-fry the spinach stems and ginger for 2 minutes. Remove from the wok.

3. Add the remaining oil to the wok. Drain the meat and reserve the marinade. Add half the meat to the wok, spreading out the slices so they do not overlap. Cook for about 3 minutes until browned on both sides. Remove from the wok and fry the remaining meat, then remove it from the wok.

4. Blend the stock and cornflour into the marinade. Add the mixture to the wok and bring to the boil. Add the spinach leaves, stems and ginger. Cook

for about 3 minutes until the spinach leaves wilt then mix in the meat. Cook for a further 1 minute and serve immediately.

Serves 4

3 | Braised Lamb

Ingredients

450 g/1 lb boned shoulder of lamb, cubed
15 ml/1 tbsp vegetable oil
4 spring onions, diagonally sliced
10 ml/2 tsp grated ginger root
300 ml/½ pt/1 ¼ cups chicken stock
30 ml/2 tbsp sugar
30 ml/2 tbsp soy sauce
15 ml/1 tbsp hoi sin sauce
15 ml/1 tbsp rice wine or dry sherry
5 ml/1 tsp sesame oil

Method

1. Blanch the lamb in boiling water for 5 minutes then drain.

2. Heat the oil in a wok over a medium heat. Stir-fry the meat for about 5 minutes until browned. Remove the meat from the wok and drain on kitchen paper.

3. Remove all but 15 ml/1 tbsp of oil from the wok. Reheat the oil, add the spring onions and ginger and stir-fry for 2 minutes.

4. Return the meat to the wok with the remaining ingredients. Bring to the boil, cover and simmer gently for 1½ hours until the meat is tender. Remove the meat from the wok and serve.

Serves 4

4 | Ginger-Spiced Beef

Ingredients

30 ml/2 tbsp white wine vinegar
10 ml/2 tsp sugar
A pinch of salt
100 g/4 oz ginger root, thinly sliced
30 ml/2 tbsp rice wine or dry sherry
10 ml/2 tsp cornflour
5 ml/1 tsp soy sauce
450 g/1 lb lean beef
45 ml/3 tbsp vegetable oil
1 large green pepper, seeded and cut into 2.5 cm/1 in pieces
6 spring onions, cut into 2.5 cm/1 in pieces
1 red chilli pepper, thinly sliced

Method

1. Mix together the vinegar, sugar and salt and stir until the sugar dissolves. Mix in the ginger and leave to stand for 30 minutes, stirring occasionally.

2. Mix together the wine or sherry, cornflour and soy sauce. Cut the meat across the grain into thin slices. Add them to the marinade, cover and leave to stand for 20 minutes, stirring occasionally.

3. Heat 30 ml/2 tbsp of the oil in a wok over a high heat. Add one-third of the meat and spread out the slices so that they do not overlap. Fry for about 3 minutes on each side until the meat is browned, then remove from the pan and fry the remaining meat.

4. Heat the remaining oil in the wok and stir-fry the pepper, spring onions, ginger mixture and marinade for about 3 minutes until the vegetables are crisp-tender. Return the meat to the wok to heat through and serve garnished with chilli.

Serves 4

5 Beef with Cashews

Ingredients

60 ml/4 tbsp vegetable oil
450 g/1 lb rump steak, thinly sliced
8 spring onions, cut into 2.5 cm/1 in pieces
2 cloves garlic, crushed
2.5 cm/1 in piece ginger root, finely chopped
75 g/3 oz/¾ cup unsalted, roasted cashews
120 ml/4 fl oz/½ cup water
20 ml/4 tsp cornflour
20 ml/4 tsp soy sauce
5 ml/1 tsp sesame oil
5 ml/1 tsp oyster sauce
5 ml/1 tsp chilli sauce

Method

1. Heat half the oil in a wok over a high heat. Stir-fry the meat a few pieces at a time for about 5 minutes until browned. Remove from the wok.

2. Heat the remaining oil and stir-fry the spring onions, garlic, ginger and cashews for 1 minute.

3. Add the meat to the wok. Mix together the water, cornflour, soy sauce, sesame oil, oyster sauce and chilli sauce. Stir this into the wok and bring to the boil, stirring until the mixture thickens. Serve immediately.

Serves 4

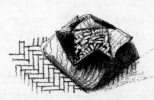

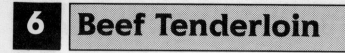

6 Beef Tenderloin

Ingredients

450 g/1 lb lean beef
45 ml/3 tbsp rice wine or dry sherry
15 ml/1 tbsp soy sauce
10 ml/2 tsp oyster sauce
5 ml/1 tsp sugar
5 ml/1 tsp cornflour
2.5 ml/½ tsp bicarbonate of soda
A pinch of salt
1 clove garlic, crushed
30 ml/2 tbsp vegetable oil
2 onions, thinly sliced

Method

1.   Cut the meat across the grain into thin slices.

2.   Mix together the wine or sherry, soy sauce, oyster sauce, sugar, cornflour, bicarbonate of soda, salt and garlic. Stir in the meat, cover and refrigerate for at least 3 hours.

3.   Heat the oil in a wok over a high heat and stir-fry the onions for about 5 minutes until golden. Transfer the onions to a warmed serving plate and keep them warm.

4.   Add one-third of the meat to the wok, spreading the slices so they do not overlap. Fry for about 3 minutes on each side until browned. Remove the meat from the pan and arrange over the onion slices. Repeat with the remaining meat.

Serves 4

7 Beef with Ginger and Garlic Noodles

Ingredients

225 g/8 oz egg noodles
120 ml/4 fl oz/½ cup beef stock
15 ml/1 tbsp soy sauce
A pinch of salt
90 ml/6 tbsp vegetable oil
450 g/1 lb rump steak, thinly sliced
6 spring onions, diagonally sliced
2.5 cm/1 in piece root ginger, thinly sliced
2 cloves garlic, crushed

Method

1. Cook the noodles according to the instructions on the packet. Drain, spread on a clean tea towel and leave to dry for 3 hours.

2. Mix together the stock, 10 ml/2 tsp of soy sauce and the salt.

3. Heat 60 ml/4 tbsp of the oil in a wok over a high heat. Stir-fry the noodles for 3 minutes. Pour in the stock mixture and toss well. Bring to the boil and cook for 2 minutes. Transfer the noodles to a warmed serving dish and keep warm.

4. Heat the remaining oil in a wok over a high heat. Add the beef, onions, ginger, garlic and remaining soy sauce. Stir-fry for about 5 minutes until the beef is cooked. Spoon the mixture over the noodles and serve immediately.

Serves 4

Beef with Satay Sauce

Ingredients

450 g/1 lb beef
75 ml/5 tbsp water
5 ml/1 tsp cornflour
15 ml/1 tbsp soy sauce
10 ml/2 tsp sesame oil
30 ml/2 tbsp vegetable oil
1 onion, coarsely chopped
1 clove garlic, crushed
15 ml/1 tbsp rice wine or dry sherry
15 ml/1 tbsp Satay Sauce (page 155)
5 ml/1 tsp curry powder
2.5 ml/½ tsp sugar
6 spring onions, thinly sliced

Method

1. Remove and discard any fat from the meat. Cut across the grain into thin slices and flatten each slice slightly by pressing with the fingers.

2. Mix together 45 ml/3 tbsp of the water with the cornflour, half the soy sauce and the sesame oil. Add the meat, stir and leave to stand for 30 minutes.

3. Heat the oil in a wok over a high heat. Add half the meat and spread out the slices so that they do not overlap. Fry for about 3 minutes on each side until light brown. Remove the meat from the wok and fry the remaining slices, then remove them from the wok.

4.   Add the onion and garlic to the wok and stir-fry for about 3 minutes until soft. Combine the remaining water and soy sauce with the wine or sherry, satay sauce, curry powder and sugar. Add the mixture to the onions and bring to the boil, stirring. Mix in the meat and heat through. Serve garnished with the spring onions.

Serves 4

Beef with Red and Green Peppers

Ingredients

450 g/1 lb lean beef
2 onions
45 ml/3 tbsp vegetable oil
1 clove garlic, crushed
A pinch of five-spice powder
1 green pepper, thinly sliced
1 red pepper, thinly sliced
25 g/1 oz mushrooms, sliced
60 ml/4 tbsp water
15 ml/1 tbsp soy sauce
5 ml/1 tsp cornflour
5 ml/1 tsp beef stock granules
5 ml/1 tsp sesame oil

Method

1. Cut the meat across the grain into thin slices. Cut the onions into wedges and separate the layers.

2. Heat the oil in a wok over a high heat. Fry the garlic and five-spice powder for 15 seconds. Add the meat and stir-fry for about 5 minutes until the meat is browned. Add the onions and stir-fry for 2 minutes. Add the mushrooms and peppers and stir-fry for about 2 minutes until the peppers are crisp-tender.

3. Combine all the remaining ingredients and pour the mixture into the wok. Cook, stirring, until the liquid boils and thickens.

Serves 4

10 Beef Curry

Ingredients

450 g/1 lb lean beef
2 onions
60 ml/4 tbsp vegetable oil
2 medium potatoes, cubed
20 ml/4 tsp curry powder
90 ml/6 tbsp chicken stock
15 ml/1 tbsp cornflour
30 ml/2 tbsp Satay Sauce (page 155)
15 ml/1 tbsp soy sauce
15 ml/1 tbsp rice wine or dry sherry
15 ml/1 tbsp chilli sauce
Steamed Rice (page 128)

Method

1. Remove and discard the fat from the meat. Cut the meat across the grain into thin slices. Cut the onions into wedges and separate the layers.

2. Heat 45 ml/3 tbsp of oil in a wok over a high heat and stir-fry the potatoes for about 5 minutes until almost tender. Add the onions and 10 ml/2 tsp of curry powder and stir-fry for 2 minutes. Remove the mixture from the wok.

3. Heat the remaining oil in the wok over a high heat. Add the meat and stir-fry until lightly browned. Add the potato mixture.

4. Combine the remaining curry powder with the stock, cornflour, satay sauce, soy sauce, wine or sherry and chilli sauce. Pour over the meat and cook, stirring, until the liquid boils. Reduce the heat and simmer for 3 minutes. Serve with the rice.

Serves 4

11 Beef with Black Bean Sauce

Ingredients

45 ml/3 tbsp soy sauce
30 ml/2 tbsp rice wine or dry sherry
15 ml/1 tbsp cornflour
1 egg white
750 g/1 ½ lb rump steak, thinly sliced
150 ml/¼ pt/⅔ cup water
30 ml/2 tbsp fermented, salted black beans
A pinch of sugar
60 ml/4 tbsp vegetable oil
4 spring onions, cut into 2.5 cm/1 in pieces
1 red pepper, seeded and thinly sliced
100 g/4 oz/½ cup bamboo shoots, sliced
5 ml/1 tsp curry powder

Method

1.   Lightly beat the soy sauce, wine or sherry, 5 ml/1
      tsp of cornflour and the egg white in a bowl. Add
      the meat, stir and leave to stand for 30 minutes,
      stirring occasionally.

2.   Mix together 90 ml/6 tbsp of the water with the
      beans and leave to stand for 15 minutes. Drain and
      reserve 5 ml/1 tsp of the water. Combine the
      beans with the reserved water and the sugar and
      mash well with a fork.

3.   Heat half the oil in a wok over a high heat. Add
      the onions, pepper, bamboo shoots and curry
      powder and stir-fry for about 2 minutes until the
      vegetables are crisp-tender. Remove from the wok.

4.   Add the remaining oil to the wok over a high heat. Add the meat and marinade and stir-fry for about 5 minutes until the meat is browned. Add the vegetables and bean mixture and mix well. Blend the remaining cornflour with the remaining water. Pour over the meat and cook, stirring, until the liquid boils and thickens.

Serves 4

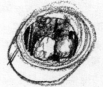

D I M   S U M

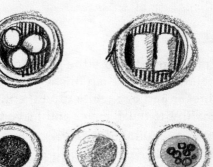

12 Beef with Celery and Ginger

Ingredients

450 g/1 lb rump steak
30 ml/2 tbsp soy sauce
5 ml/1 tsp white wine vinegar
1 egg white
4 sticks celery, diagonally sliced
375 ml/13 fl oz/1 ½ cups water
2.5 ml/½ tsp salt
45 ml/3 tbsp vegetable oil
6 spring onions, cut into 2.5 cm/1 in pieces
15 ml/1 tbsp finely chopped ginger root
1 clove garlic, crushed
30 ml/2 tbsp rice wine or dry sherry
15 ml/1 tbsp cornflour
10 ml/2 tsp oyster sauce

Method

1.   Cut the meat across the grain into thin strips. Beat together 10 ml/2 tsp of soy sauce with the wine vinegar and egg white until the mixture is foamy. Mix in the meat, cover and leave to stand for 1 hour, stirring occasionally.

2.   Place the celery, 250 ml/8 fl oz/1 cup of water and the salt in a saucepan, bring to the boil and boil for 3 minutes. Drain.

3.   Heat 30 ml/2 tbsp of oil in a wok over a high heat. Drain the meat and add it to the wok. Stir-fry for about 5 minutes until the meat is browned. Remove the meat from the wok.

4.   Add the remaining oil to the wok and heat. Add the celery, spring onions, ginger and garlic and

stir-fry for 1 minute. Stir in the meat.

5.   Mix together the remaining water, the wine or
      sherry, cornflour and oyster sauce. Pour into the
      wok and cook, stirring, until the mixture boils and
      thickens.

Serves 4

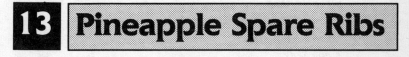

13 Pineapple Spare Ribs

Ingredients

1 kg/2 ¼ lb pork spare ribs, cut into 5 cm/2 in lengths
1 x 300 g/12 oz can pineapple, drained and crushed
30 ml/2 tbsp soy sauce
60 ml/4 tbsp vegetable oil
60 ml/4 tbsp tomato purée
30 ml/2 tbsp hoi sin sauce
1 x 2.5 cm/1 in piece ginger root
5 ml/1 tsp lemon juice
Salt and freshly ground black pepper

Method

1.   Place the spare ribs in a large saucepan and just
      cover with water. Bring to the boil and simmer for
      10 minutes, then drain well.

2.   Mix together all the remaining ingredients, add the
      pork and marinate for at least 1 hour.

3.   Spread the spare ribs over a baking tin and spoon
      some of the marinade over the top. Bake in a
      preheated oven at 180°C/350°F/gas mark 4 for
      about 1 hour, basting occasionally with the
      remaining marinade.

Serves 4

14 | Sweet and Sour Pork

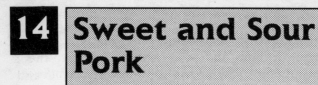

Ingredients

1.2 kg/2 ½ lb lean pork chops
60 ml/4 tbsp soy sauce
30 ml/2 tbsp rice wine or dry sherry
10 ml/2 tsp sugar
1 egg yolk
75 g/3 oz/¾ cup cornflour
750 ml/1 ¼ pts/3 cups vegetable oil
1 large onion, thinly sliced
8 spring onions, diagonally sliced
1 red or green pepper, seeded and chopped
100 g/4 oz mushrooms, halved or quartered
2 sticks celery, diagonally sliced
1 cucumber, seeded and chopped
1 x 450 g/1 lb can pineapple chunks in syrup
60 ml/4 tbsp white wine vinegar
45 ml/3 tbsp tomato sauce
250 ml/8 fl oz/1 cup water

Method

1.   Trim the chops, discard the fat and bones. Cut the
        pork into 2.5 cm/1 in pieces. Mix together the soy
        sauce, wine or sherry, sugar and egg yolk. Mix in
        the pork, cover and leave to stand for 1 hour,
        stirring occasionally.

2.   Drain the pork, reserving the marinade. Reserve 30
        ml/2 tbsp of cornflour and use the remainder to
        coat the pork. Reserve 45 ml/3 tbsp of oil and heat
        the remainder in a wok over a high heat until very
        hot. Fry half the pork in the oil for about 5
        minutes until browned. Drain on kitchen paper.
        Fry and drain the remaining pork.

3. Heat the reserved oil in a wok over a high heat. Add the onion, spring onions, pepper, mushrooms, celery and cucumber and stir-fry for 3 minutes.

4. Drain the pineapple, reserving the syrup. Mix the syrup with the marinade, wine vinegar and tomato sauce and add this to the wok. Mix the water with the remaining cornflour and add this to the wok. Cook, stirring, until the sauce boils and thickens. Add the pork and pineapple and cook, stirring, until heated through.

Serves 6

15 Barbecued Pork

Ingredients

2 whole pork tenderloins
   (about 350 g/12 oz each)
30 ml/2 tbsp red wine
15 ml/1 tbsp brown sugar
15 ml/1 tbsp honey
60 ml/4 tbsp soy sauce
2 ml/½ tbsp powdered cinnamon
10 ml/2 tsp cochineal (red colouring)
   (may be omitted)
1 clove of garlic
1 green onion cut into ⅛ths.

Method

1. Remove the fat and use only the lean meat.

2. Mix together in a bowl your wine, sugar, honey, garlic, cinnamon, soy sauce and onion. Add the meat and fully coat it with the mixture.

3. Cover the bowl and let the meat marinate for at least an hour. But turn the meat over a couple of times.

4. Preheat your oven to 180°C/350°F. Drain the meat. Place it on a wire rack in the baking pan and cook for about 45 minutes. Keep turning the tenderloin regularly and baste them during this roasting. Cut into thin slices to serve.

Serves 4

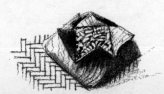

16 Spicy Pork with Pickles

Ingredients

1.2 kg/2 ½ lb lean pork chops
30 ml/2 tbsp cornflour
45 ml/3 tbsp soy sauce
30 ml/2 tbsp sweet sherry
5 ml/1 tsp grated ginger root
2.5 ml/½ tsp five-spice powder
A pinch of freshly ground black pepper
750 ml/1 ¼ pts/3 cups vegetable oil
60 ml/4 tbsp chicken stock
Chinese Mixed Pickles (page 126)

Method

1. Trim the chops, discarding the fat and bones. Mix together the cornflour, 30 ml/2 tbsp of the soy sauce, the sherry, ginger, five-spice powder and pepper. Add the pork, a piece at a time, turning to coat it completely. Cover and leave to stand for 2 hours, stirring occasionally.

2. Heat the oil in a wok over a high heat until very hot. Cook the pork a few pieces at a time for about 5 minutes until browned and cooked through. Drain on kitchen paper.

3. Cut the pork into thick slices, transfer to a warmed serving dish and keep warm.

4. Mix together the stock and remaining soy sauce in a small saucepan. Bring to the boil and pour over the sliced pork. Serve garnished with mixed pickles.

Serves 4

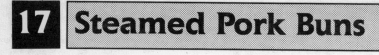

17 Steamed Pork Buns

Ingredients

30 ml/2 tbsp hoi sin sauce
15 ml/1 tbsp oyster sauce
15 ml/1 tbsp soy sauce
2.5 ml/½ tsp sesame oil
30 ml/2 tbsp vegetable oil
10 ml/2 tsp grated ginger root
1 clove garlic, crushed
300 ml/½ pt/1 ¼ cups water
15 ml/1 tbsp cornflour
225 g/8 oz Barbecued Pork (page 114), finely chopped
4 spring onions, finely chopped
350 g/12 oz/3 cups plain flour
15 ml/1 tbsp baking powder
2.5 ml/½ tsp salt
50 g/2 oz/¼ cup lard
5 ml/1 tsp white wine vinegar
12 x 13 cm/5 in greaseproof paper squares

Method

1. Mix together the hoi sin sauce, oyster sauce, soy sauce and sesame oil.

2. Heat the vegetable oil in a wok over a high heat. Stir-fry the ginger and garlic for 1 minute. Stir in the hoi sin mixture and cook, stirring, for 2 minutes.

3. Blend 120 ml/4 fl oz/½ cup of water with the cornflour and stir it into the wok. Cook, stirring, until the mixture boils then simmer for 2 minutes. Stir in the pork and onions. Remove from the heat and leave to cool.

4. Mix together the flour, baking powder and salt. Rub in the lard until the mixture resembles fine breadcrumbs. Mix the wine vinegar into the remaining water. Mix this into the flour to form a firm dough. Knead lightly on a floured surface, then cover and leave to stand for 20 minutes.

5. Uncover the dough and knead again. Divide into 12 equal portions and shape each into a smooth ball. Roll each ball on a lightly floured surface into a circle 15 cm/6 in in diameter. Brush around the edges lightly with water. Place spoonfuls of the pork mixture on to the centre of each circle. Carefully pinch the edges together to seal the dough around the filling. Bring the two ends of the dough over the seam and pinch together.

6. Brush one side of each greaseproof paper square with oil. Place each bun on a square of paper, seam side down. Place the buns in a single layer on a steamer rack over boiling water. Cover and steam the buns for about 20 minutes until cooked.

Makes 12

Chapter 7

Vegetables

*The Chinese like to offer a
balanced selection of dishes to
their guests. These vegetable
dishes will give you a good
choice to accompany the meat
and fish dishes you wish to
serve.*

1 Chinese Asparagus

Ingredients

600 ml/1 pt/2 ½ cups water
450 g/1 lb asparagus, trimmed
30 ml/2 tbsp cornflour
5 ml/1 tsp grated ginger root
10 ml/2 tsp sugar
45 ml/3 tbsp soy sauce
Salt and freshly ground black pepper

Method

1. Bring the water to the boil in a large saucepan. Add the asparagus and simmer for 10 minutes. Drain the asparagus and keep it warm, reserving the cooking stock. Return the cooking stock to the pan.

2. Blend the cornflour with a little of the stock. Bring the remaining stock to the boil, then stir in the ginger, sugar, soy sauce and cornflour. Season to taste with salt and pepper. Boil, uncovered, for 5 minutes to reduce slightly and serve with the asparagus.

Serves 4

2 Spicy Mushrooms

Ingredients

15 ml/1 tbsp vegetable oil
1 clove garlic, finely chopped
5 ml/1 tsp grated ginger root
2 spring onions, finely chopped
225 g/8 oz button mushrooms
15 ml/1 tbsp hoi sin sauce
15 ml/1 tbsp rice wine or dry sherry
15 ml/1 tbsp soy sauce
45 ml/3 tbsp chicken stock
5 ml/1 tsp sesame oil

Method

1. Heat the oil in a wok over a medium heat and stir-fry the garlic, ginger and spring onions for 1 minute.

2. Add the mushrooms and stir-fry for 1 minute, then add the remaining ingredients and stir-fry for a further 5 minutes. Serve immediately.

Serves 4

3 Mushrooms and Bamboo Shoots

Ingredients

60 ml/4 tbsp vegetable oil
175 g/6 oz mushrooms, sliced
350 g/12 oz/1 ½ cups bamboo shoots, thinly sliced
300 ml/½ pt/1 ¼ cups chicken stock

45 ml/3 tbsp soy sauce
45 ml/3 tbsp rice wine or dry sherry
10 ml/2 tsp sugar
Salt and freshly ground black pepper
15 ml/1 tbsp cornflour

Method

1. Heat the oil in a wok over a medium heat and stir-fry the mushrooms and bamboo shoots for 5 minutes. Add the stock, soy sauce, wine or sherry and sugar and season to taste with salt and pepper. Bring to the boil and simmer for 5 minutes.

2. Blend the cornflour with a little cold water and stir it into the wok. Cook for a further 3 minutes.

Serves 4

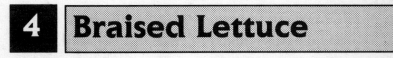

4 Braised Lettuce

Ingredients

1 head crisp lettuce
15 ml/1 tbsp vegetable oil
2.5 ml/½ tsp salt
1 clove garlic, crushed
60 ml/4 tbsp chicken or vegetable stock
5 ml/1 tsp soy sauce

Method

1. Separate the lettuce into leaves and wash thoroughly.

2. Heat the oil in a wok over a medium heat. Add the salt and garlic and fry for a few minutes until the garlic begins to brown. Add the lettuce and stir-fry for 1 minute.

3. Add the stock and stir-fry for a further 2 minutes. Serve sprinkled with soy sauce.

Serves 4

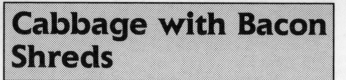

5 | Cabbage with Bacon Shreds

Ingredients

1 small head green cabbage, finely shredded
Salt
3 slices streaky bacon, rinded and cut into thin strips
30 ml/2 tbsp vegetable oil
2 cloves garlic, crushed
5 ml/1 tsp grated ginger root
5 ml/1 tsp sugar
120 ml/4 fl oz/½ cup chicken or vegetable stock

Method

1. Sprinkle the cabbage with salt and leave to stand.

2. Fry the bacon until just crisp, then set aside.

3. Heat the oil in a wok over a medium heat and fry the garlic for a few minutes until browned, then remove them from the wok and discard.

4. Add the cabbage, ginger and sugar and stir-fry for 2 minutes. Add the stock and bacon and stir-fry for a further 2 minutes. Serve with fried rice.

Serves 4

6 | Spinach with Garlic

Ingredients

30 ml/2 tbsp vegetable oil
450 g/1 lb spinach leaves
2.5 ml/½ tsp salt
1 clove garlic, finely chopped
15 ml/1 tbsp soy sauce

Method

1. Heat the oil in a wok over a medium heat. Add the spinach and salt and stir-fry for 3 minutes.

2. Add the remaining ingredients and stir-fry for a further 4 minutes. Serve immediately.

Serves 4

7 **Bean Sprout and Salami Salad**

Ingredients

350 g/12 oz/¾ lb bean sprouts
225 g/8 oz salami
30 ml/2 tbsp lemon juice
90 ml/6 tbsp vegetable oil
Salt
2.5 ml/½ tsp mustard
2.5 ml/½ tsp sugar
2.5 ml/½ tsp sesame oil
2.5 ml/½ tsp soy sauce

Method

1. Remove the ends from the bean sprouts and wash thoroughly. Plunge them into boiling water for 1 minute, then remove and drain.

2. Place the bean sprouts in a salad bowl and arrange the salami slices on top. Chill until required.

3. Mix all the remaining ingredients together well in a screw-top jar and chill.

4. Just before serving, pour the dressing over the salad and toss gently.

Serves 4

8 | Mixed Vegetables

Ingredients

450 g/1 lb broccoli
2 onions
30 ml/2 tbsp vegetable oil
15 ml/1 tbsp grated ginger root
225 g/8 oz spinach, chopped
225 g/8 oz mangetout
4 sticks celery, diagonally sliced
8 spring onions, diagonally sliced
175 ml/6 fl oz/¾ cup chicken or vegetable stock

Method

1.   Cut the broccoli into small florets and the stalks into thin strips. Cut the onions into wedges and separate the layers.

2.   Heat the oil in a wok over a high heat and stir-fry the broccoli, onion and ginger for 1 minute. Add the remaining vegetables and toss lightly.

3.   Add the stock and toss until the vegetables are completely coated. Bring to the boil, cover and simmer for about 3 minutes until the vegetables are crisp-tender.

4.   As a variation, you can add sliced carrots, courgettes, green beans or green peppers in addition or instead of the listed vegetables.

Serves 4

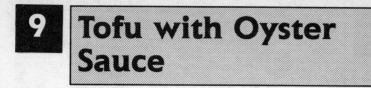

9 Tofu with Oyster Sauce

Ingredients

30 ml/2 tbsp vegetable oil
225 g/8 oz/1 cup tofu, cubed
225 g/8 oz mushrooms, sliced
6 spring onions, cut into 2.5 cm/1 in pieces
3 sticks celery, sliced
1 red or green pepper, seeded and cut into chunks
120 ml/4 fl oz/½ cup water
15 ml/1 tbsp cornflour
30 ml/2 tbsp oyster sauce
20 ml/4 tsp rice wine or dry sherry
20 ml/4 tsp soy sauce

Method

1. Heat half the oil and fry the tofu for about 3 minutes until lightly browned, stirring gently. Remove from the wok.

2. Heat the remaining oil and stir-fry the mushrooms, spring onions, celery and pepper for 1 minute.

3. Return the tofu to the wok and toss lightly to combine the ingredients. Blend the water, cornflour, oyster sauce, wine or sherry and soy sauce. Pour the mixture into the wok and bring to the boil, stirring continuously. Cook, stirring, for a further 1 minute. Serve immediately.

Serves 4

10 Chinese Mixed Pickles

Ingredients

750 g/1 lb 8 oz/3 cups sugar
750 ml/1 ¼ pts/3 cups white wine vinegar
375 ml/13 fl oz/1 ½ cups water
10 ml/2 tsp salt
3 large carrots, cut into julienne strips
1 Chinese radish, cut into julienne strips
1 large cucumber, cut into julienne strips
4 sticks celery, thinly sliced
8 spring onions, diagonally sliced
1 large red pepper, seeded and cubed
1 large green pepper, seeded and cubed
100 g/4 oz ginger root, thinly sliced

Method

1. Mix together the sugar, wine vinegar, water and salt in a large saucepan. Bring to the boil over a medium heat, stirring, then remove from the heat and leave to cool.

2. Bring a large saucepan of water to the boil. Add the vegetables and remove from the heat immediately. Leave to stand, uncovered, for 2 minutes. Drain well. Spread the vegetables out on a clean tea towel and leave to dry for 2 or 3 hours.

3. Pack the vegetables firmly into clean jars with plastic lids. Do not use metal lids as the vinegar will corrode the metal. Pour the pickling liquid into the jars until the vegetables are completely covered. Seal and store in the refrigerator for at least 1 week before using.

Makes 1.5 litres/3 pts/7 ½ cups

Rice and
Noodles

*Rice and noodles are traditional
accompaniments to a Chinese
meal. Choose a simple or more
strongly flavoured dish to suit the
other dishes you are serving.*

1 Steamed Rice

Ingredients

> 225 g/8 oz/1 cup long-grained rice, rinsed
> 450 ml/¾ pt/2 cups water
> 5 ml/1 tsp salt
> 15 ml/1 tbsp vegetable oil

Method

1. Place all the ingredients in a large saucepan and bring to the boil over a medium heat. Cover and simmer for about 15 minutes until the rice is tender.

2. Remove the pan from the heat and leave to stand for 5 minutes. Uncover and fluff the rice with a fork.

Serves 4

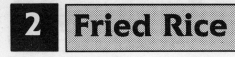

2 Fried Rice

Ingredients

375/13 fl oz/1 ½ cups water
5 ml/1 tsp salt
175 g/6 oz/¾ cup long-grain rice
2 slices bacon, chopped
3 eggs
A pinch of freshly ground black pepper
5 ml/1 tsp grated ginger root
100 g/4 oz cooked pork, cut into thin strips
100 g/4 oz shelled prawns, coarsely chopped
4 spring onions, finely chopped
15 ml/1 tbsp soy sauce

Method

1. Bring the water and salt to the boil in a large saucepan. Stir in the rice, cover and simmer for about 15 minutes until the rice is tender. Drain.

2. Fry the bacon in a wok over a medium heat, stirring frequently, until crisp. Drain. Remove all but 15 ml/1 tbsp of fat from the wok.

3. Beat the eggs and pepper. Pour one-third of the egg into the wok, tilting the wok so that it covers the bottom. Cook over a medium heat for about 3 minutes until the eggs are set. Remove from the wok, roll up and cut into thin strips. Using a little more oil, repeat with the remaining eggs.

4. Add the remaining oil to the wok and stir-fry the ginger over a medium heat for 1 minute. Stir in the rice. Add the bacon, pork, prawns, onions and soy sauce and stir-fry for 3 minutes until heated through.

Serves 4

3 Chicken Liver Rice

Ingredients

175 g/6 oz/¾ cup long-grain rice
375 ml/13 fl oz/1 ½ cups chicken stock
Salt
2 cooked chicken livers, thinly sliced

Method

1. Place the rice and stock in a large saucepan and bring to the boil. Cover and simmer for about 15 minutes.

2. When most of the stock has been absorbed, stir in salt to taste and add the chicken livers. Simmer gently to heat through.

Serves 4

4 Almond Fried Rice

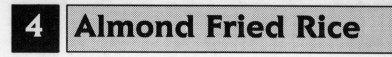

Ingredients

450 g/1 lb/4 cups cooked long-grain rice
250 ml/8 fl oz/1 cup vegetable oil
50 g/2 oz/½ cup flaked almonds
4 eggs, beaten
5 ml/1 tsp salt
3 slices cooked ham, cut into strips
2 shallots, finely chopped
15 ml/1 tbsp soy sauce

Method

1. Separate the rice grains with a fork.

2. Heat the oil in a wok over a medium heat and fry the almonds for a few minutes until golden. Remove from the wok and drain on kitchen paper.

3. Drain most of the oil from the wok and heat up again. Pour in the eggs, stirring continuously, then immediately add the rice and salt. Cook the rice for 5 minutes, lifting and stirring quickly so that the rice grains are coated in the egg.

4. Stir in the ham, shallots and soy sauce and cook for a further 2 minutes.

5. Fold in most of the almonds and serve garnished with the remaining almonds.

Serves 4

5 | Fried Tuna Rice

Ingredients

30 ml/2 tbsp vegetable oil
2 onions, sliced
1 green pepper, chopped
450 g/1 lb/4 cups cooked long-grain rice
Salt
3 eggs, beaten
1 x 300 g/12 oz can tuna, flaked
30 ml/2 tbsp soy sauce
2 shallots, finely chopped

Method

1. Heat the oil in a wok over a medium heat and fry the onions until soft. Add the pepper and fry for a further 1 minute. Push to one side of the wok.

2. Add the rice to the wok, sprinkle with salt and stir-fry for 5 minutes, gradually mixing in the onions and pepper.

3. Make a well in the centre of the rice, pour in a little more oil, and pour in the eggs. Stir until almost scrambled and mix in with the rice. Cook for a further 3 minutes.

4. Add the tuna and soy sauce and heat through thoroughly.

5. Serve garnished with chopped shallots.

Serves 4

6 Rice Vermicelli

Ingredients

225 g/8 oz Chinese rice vermicelli
750 ml/1 ¼ pts/3 cups vegetable oil

Method

1. Gently pull the vermicelli apart into small bunches.

2. Heat the oil in a wok over a medium heat. Using long-handled tongs or spoons, place a bunch of vermicelli in the hot oil and cook for about 5 seconds until it rises to the top. Remove from the wok and drain on kitchen paper. Repeat with the remaining vermicelli.

3. Serve separately or as a side dish with other foods.

Serves 4

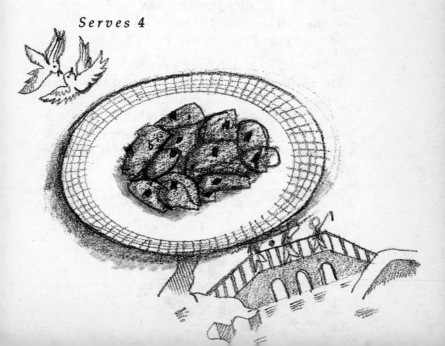

Noodle Baskets

Ingredients

225 g/8 oz thin egg noodles
Salt
750 ml/1 ¼ pts/3 cups vegetable oil

Method

1. Cook the noodles in boiling salted water according to the instructions on the packet. Drain well.

2. Arrange several layers of kitchen paper over a baking sheet, spread out the noodles and leave them to dry for at least 8 hours.

3. Brush the inside of a medium-sized strainer with a little of the oil. Spread an even layer of noodles about 1.5 cm/½ in thick in the strainer. Brush the outside of a smaller strainer with oil. Place the second strainer, rounded side down, over the noodles in the first strainer. Press lightly.

4. Heat the oil in a wok over a medium heat. Carefully lower the two strainers into the oil and fry for about 2 minutes until the noodles are golden. Remove from the oil and drain on kitchen paper. Carefully remove the strainers, running a knife around the edge of the noodles if necessary to loosen them. Drain on kitchen paper.

Makes 6-8 baskets

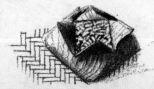

8 Fried Noodles

Ingredients

225 g/8 oz thin egg noodles
Salt
750 ml/1 ¼ pts/3 cups vegetable oil

Method

1. Cook the noodles in boiling salted water according to the instructions on the packet. Drain well.

2. Arrange several layers of kitchen paper over a baking sheet, spread out the noodles and leave them to dry for 2 to 3 hours.

3. Heat the oil in a wok over a medium-high heat. Using long-handled tongs or a slotted spoon, fry small amounts of noodles at a time in the oil for about 30 seconds until golden. Remove the noodles from the wok and drain on kitchen paper.

Serves 4

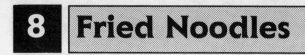

Noodle Salad

Ingredients

225 g/8 oz thin egg noodles
15 ml/1 tbsp sesame oil
3 eggs, beaten
30 ml/2 tbsp vegetable oil
100 g/4 oz cooked chicken, cut into strips
100 g/4 oz crabmeat, flaked
3 slices cooked ham, cut into strips
30 ml/2 tbsp soy sauce
Salt and freshly ground black pepper
2 shallots, finely chopped

Method

1. Cook the noodles in boiling water according to the directions on the packet. Drain well then stir in the sesame oil.

2. Heat a small omelette pan and fry one-third of the eggs to make an omelette. Remove from the pan, roll up and cut into thin strips. Repeat with the remaining egg.

3. Heat the oil in a wok over a medium heat. Add the noodles and stir-fry for 3 minutes. Add the meats, omelette strips and soy sauce, stir together gently. Season to taste with salt and pepper.

4. Transfer to a serving dish and sprinkle with the chopped shallots. Cool and refrigerate for 1 hour before serving.

Serves 4

10 Chinese Pancakes

Ingredients

175 g/6 oz/1 ½ cups plain flour
120 ml/4 fl oz/½ cup hot water
15 ml/1 tbsp sesame oil

Method

1. Place the flour in a large bowl. Gradually mix in the water to form a dough, adding a little more hot water if necessary. Knead well for 5 minutes then cover with a damp cloth and leave to stand for 30 minutes.

2. Knead the dough again until smooth. Roll into a sausage shape and cut into about 10 equal pieces. Roll each piece into a ball.

3. Brush one side of a ball with sesame oil and press the oiled side on to a second ball. Roll out the two together to a 15 cm/6 in circle. Roll the other pancakes in the same way.

4. Heat a frying pan over a low heat and place one double pancake in the pan. Heat for a few minutes until the underside has dried, then turn the pancake and dry the other side. Repeat with the remaining pancakes.

5. Steam the pancakes in a bamboo steamer to reheat them.

Serves 4

Desserts

*There is a small range of desserts
in Chinese cuisine. This selection
includes those which are most
traditional with other delicious
desserts which make a superb
ending to a Chinese meal.*

1 Banana Fritters

Ingredients

175 g/6 oz/1 ½ cups plain flour
5 ml/1 tsp baking powder
A pinch of bicarbonate of soda
A pinch of salt
175 ml/6 fl oz/¾ cup water
4 firm bananas
750 ml/1 ¼ pts/3 cups vegetable oil

Method

1. Mix together 100 g/4 oz/1 cup of flour with the baking powder, bicarbonate of soda and salt.

2. Gradually blend in the water, beating with a whisk until smooth.

3. Peel the bananas. Cut each one crosswise into 3 pieces. Coat the bananas lightly with the remaining flour.

4. Heat the oil in a wok over a medium heat. Dip the banana pieces in the batter, coating completely. Fry them a few at a time for about 5 minutes until golden. Drain on kitchen paper and serve with ice-cream.

Serves 4

2   Toffee Apples

Ingredients

2 medium cooking apples
100 g/4 oz/1 cup plain flour
450 ml/¾ pt/2 cups water
15 ml/1 tbsp sesame oil
750 ml/1 ¼ pts/3 cups vegetable oil
450 g/1 lb/2 cups sugar
30 ml/2 tbsp sesame seeds
Cold water
Ice cubes

Method

1.   Peel and core the apples and cut into quarters. Cut each quarter in half crosswise, making 16 pieces.

2.   Measure the flour into a bowl and gradually whisk in half the water. Add 10 ml/2 tsp of the sesame oil and beat until smooth.

3.   Brush the remaining sesame oil over a serving plate and set aside.

4.   Place the apple pieces in the batter, turning to coat them completely.

5.   Heat the vegetable oil in a wok over a medium heat until hot. Lift the apple pieces from the batter using a slotted spoon and fry them a few at a time for about 3 minutes until light brown. Remove from the wok and drain on kitchen paper.

6.   Pour the oil out of the wok but do not clean it. Pour the remaining water and the sugar into the wok and bring to the boil. Simmer, stirring constantly, until the mixture reaches about 113°C/235°F.

7.   Remove from the heat immediately, mix in the
        apples and sesame seeds, transfer to the oiled
        serving plate and serve immediately with a bowl of
        iced water in which to dunk the apples before
        eating.

        Serves 4

3 **Water Melon in Wine**

Ingredients

½ water melon
250 ml/8 fl oz/1 cup water
125 ml/4 fl oz/½ cup ginger wine
30 ml/2 tbsp sugar
25 g/1 oz preserved candied ginger, cut into thin slivers

Method

1.   Shape the water melon into balls using a melon
        baller, removing the seeds as necessary.

2.   Mix together the water, ginger wine and sugar in a
        small saucepan. Cook over a medium heat, stirring
        until the sugar dissolves and the mixture is hot.
        Remove from the heat.

3.   Stir the ginger into the wine mixture. Pour over
        the melon balls and refrigerate for several hours,
        preferably overnight.

        Serves 4

4 Mandarin-Liqueur Sorbet with Lychees

Ingredients

450 ml/¾ pt/2 cups water
100 g/4 oz/½ cup sugar
2 x 300 g/11 oz cans mandarin orange segments in syrup
60 ml/4 tbsp lemon juice
30 ml/2 tbsp orange liqueur
1 x 500 g/1 lb 2 oz can lychees in syrup

Method

1. Place the water and sugar in a medium saucepan and cook over a low heat, stirring continuously until the mixture boils. Boil, stirring, for 3 minutes. Remove from the heat and leave to cool.

2. Purée 1 can of mandarins with their syrup until smooth. Strain.

3. Stir the purée, lemon juice and liqueur into the cooled syrup. Pour into a 1.5 litre/2 ½ pt/6 cup baking dish and freeze for at least 3 hours until firm. Refrigerate the remaining mandarins and the lychees until cold.

4. To serve, drain the mandarins and lychees, reserving the lychee syrup. Spoon the fruit and lychee syrup into serving dishes. Remove the frozen mixture from the freezer and flake it lightly with a fork. Spoon over the fruit and serve.

Serves 4

5 Raspberry Sorbet

Ingredients

375 g/12 oz raspberries
250 ml/8 fl oz/1 cup water
175 g/6 oz/¾ cup caster sugar
30 ml/2 tbsp lemon juice
30 ml/2 tbsp orange liqueur
2 egg whites
A pinch of cream of tartar

Method

1. Wash and hull the raspberries and purée them with the water, half the sugar, the lemon juice and liqueur.

2. Strain into a baking tin and freeze for about 4 hours until firm.

3. Beat the egg whites and cream of tartar until foamy. Gradually add the remaining sugar and whisk until the whites are stiff but not dry.

4. Remove the raspberry mixture from the freezer and flake it with a fork. Spoon the egg whites over the top and fold them into the raspberry mixture gently but thoroughly. Freeze for at least 2 hours until firm.

Serves 6

6 | Champagne Melon

Ingredients

1 small honeydew melon
120 ml/4 fl oz/½ cup water
100 g/4 oz/½ cup sugar
60 ml/4 tbsp ginger wine
1 bottle Champagne or sparkling wine
450 g/1 lb seedless green grapes
1 egg white
225 g/8 oz/1 cup caster sugar

Method

1.   Cut the melon in half and remove the seeds. Shape the melon into balls using a melon baller. Place the melon balls in a bowl, cover with clingfilm and refrigerate until cold.

2.   Mix together the water, sugar and ginger wine in a small saucepan and cook at a medium heat, stirring until the sugar dissolves. Bring to the boil and boil for 3 minutes then remove the pan from the heat. Leave to cool and refrigerate until cold.

3.   Refrigerate the Champagne or sparkling wine until cold.

4.   Cut the grapes into 6 small bunches, leaving a large enough stem section on each to hook over the rim of a glass.

5.   Beat the egg white until frothy. Brush over the grapes, then immediately place the grapes in the caster sugar, turning to coat them completely. Place the grapes on a large plate and leave to stand for 2 hours.

6.   Divide the melon balls between 6 large wine glasses. Spoon about 30 ml/2 tbsp of the ginger

syrup over each glass. Fill the glasses with Champagne or sparkling wine. Hang a bunch of grapes over the outside edge of each glass and serve immediately.

Serves 6

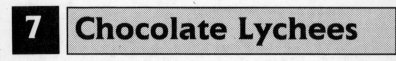

7 Chocolate Lychees

Ingredients

1 x 500 g/1 lb 2 oz can lychees, drained
175 g/6 oz chocolate
15 ml/1 tbsp vegetable fat

Method

1. Spread the lychees round side up between several layers of kitchen paper. Leave to stand for about 1 hour until dry.

2. Melt the chocolate and fat in the top of a double saucepan over boiling water. Remove from the heat and leave to cool slightly.

3. Dip each lychee in chocolate to coat it completely. Carefully lift the lychees out of the chocolate and place round side up on greased baking parchment or greaseproof paper. Drizzle the remaining chocolate over the lychees and refrigerate until cold.

Makes 24

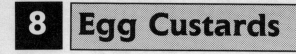

8 Egg Custards

Ingredients

> 375 g/12 oz/3 cups plain flour
> 5 ml/1 tsp salt
> 225 g/8 oz/1 cup lard or vegetable fat
> 60-90 ml/4-6 tbsp hot tap water
> 3 eggs
> 75 g/3 oz/⅓ cup sugar
> 375 ml/13 fl oz/1 ½ cups milk

Method

1. Mix together the flour and half the salt and rub in the lard until the mixture resembles breadcrumbs. Mix in enough water to form a soft dough. Cut the dough in half.

2. Roll out each half on a lightly floured surface to 5 mm/⅛ in thick. Cut out 12 x 8 cm/3 in circles. Press the circles into greased muffin tins.

3. Beat the eggs and stir in the sugar and remaining salt. Gradually blend in the milk. Spoon the mixture into the pastry cases and bake in a preheated oven at 180°C/350°F/gas mark 4 for about 30 minutes until a knife inserted into the centre of the tarts comes out clean. Remove from the tins and cool on a wire rack.

Makes 24

Fruits with Almond Cream

Ingredients

175 ml/6 fl oz/¾ cup water
1 sachet gelatine
100 g/4 oz/½ cup sugar
175 ml/6 fl oz/¾ cup boiling water
300 ml/½ pt/1 ¼ cups evaporated milk
2.5 ml/½ tsp vanilla essence
2.5 ml/½ tsp almond essence
2 kiwi fruits, peeled and sliced
4 strawberries

Method

1. Measure the cold water into a bowl, sprinkle on the gelatine and leave to stand for 1 minute. Add the sugar and stir until the gelatine dissolves.

2. Stir the gelatine mixture into the boiling water. Mix together the milk, vanilla essence and almond essence and pour into the gelatine mixture.

3. Divide the mixture between 4 serving dishes and refrigerate for about 3 hours until set. Serve garnished with the kiwi fruits and strawberries.

Serves 4

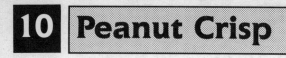

10 Peanut Crisp

Ingredients

50 g/2 oz/½ cup sesame seeds
450 g/1 lb/2 cups sugar
75 ml/5 tbsp white wine vinegar
20 ml/4 tbsp water
225 g/8 oz/1 ½ cups roasted unsalted skinned peanuts

Method

1. Sprinkle the sesame seeds evenly into a large baking tin and bake in a preheated oven at 180°C/350°F/gas mark 4 for about 5 minutes. Leave to cool.

2. Mix the sugar, wine vinegar and water in a medium saucepan and cook over a low heat, stirring until the sugar dissolves. Bring to the boil without stirring. Boil, without stirring, for about 10 minutes until the mixture is golden and reaches 149°C/300°F or hard-crack stage.

3. While the sugar is boiling, grease a large baking tin. Sprinkle half the sesame seeds and all the peanuts evenly into the tin.

4. Pour the sugar mixture over the nuts and smooth the surface with the back of a greased wooden spoon. Sprinkle with the remaining sesame seeds and leave to cool slightly. While still warm, cut into 5 cm/2 in squares. Leave to cool completely then remove from the tin.

Makes 24 to 36

Drinks

China Tea

For over a thousand years, tea has been the drink of China. The Chinese drink it at any time of day, before, during or after meals. They never interfere with the tea's natural flavour by adding sugar, lemon, cream or milk.

There are many varieties of Chinese tea that differ greatly in character, flavour and aroma. Since the leaves for all Chinese teas come from the same place, the differences are a result of the processing techniques.

1. Green Tea

This is an unfermented tea that produces a light golden drink. Its leaves retain their natural green colour and its taste is delicate. It is suitable for drinking at any time of day with most foods.

2. Black Tea

This is a fermented tea that produces a full-bodied brew. Its leaves change colour during fermentation from green to red to black. It's a good choice for accompanying full-flavoured, spicy dishes and deep-fried foods. Among the black teas, the most popular include Keemun and Lapsang Souchong.

3. Oolong Tea

A semi-fermented tea, this yields an amber brew. It combines the more pungent aroma of the black teas and the delicate fragrance of the green teas. The fermentation process is stopped midway, producing leaves that are brownish-green. Oolong tea is a good choice with distinctively flavoured foods such as shrimp, fish, broccoli and cauliflower.

4. Scented Tea

A blend of tea leaves and fresh or dried flowers, scented teas can be made from green, black or oolong varieties. They are good with many stir-fried dishes and are especially nice between meals. The most popular scented teas are jasmine, lychee and chrysanthemum.

5. Brewing China Tea

There is no exact recipe for making Chinese teas. The amount required to brew a cup varies with the variety and the nature of each tea. Unlike many other teas, the colour of Chinese tea is not a good indicator of its strength of flavour. It is usually stronger than its colour suggests. A general guide is to use 2-5 ml/½-1 tsp of tea for each 250 ml/8 fl oz/1 cup of water. Green teas are more potent than other varieties and should be used in smaller amounts.

Tea is generally made in a clean china, not a metal, teapot. To brew the tea, scald the inside of the pot with boiling water, then discard the water. Add the tea leaves to the pot and pour in boiling water. Cover the pot and let it stand for 3 to 5 minutes. Time the tea. Do not attempt to judge whether it is done by its colour.

Most Chinese teas can be infused more than once. In fact, many believe that the flavour of the second infusion is superior to the first. Simply pour fresh boiling water over the tea leaves in the pot without adding additional leaves.

6 Almond Tea

Ingredients

450 g/1 lb shelled almonds
45 ml/3 tbsp vegetable oil
500 ml/18 fl oz/2 ¼ cups water
100 g/4 oz/½ cup sugar
A pinch of salt
45 ml/3 tbsp cornflour

Method

1. Place the almonds in a saucepan and just cover with water. Bring to the boil, simmer for 10 minutes, then strain and allow to cool.

2. Heat the oil in a wok over a medium heat and fry the almonds until golden. Remove from the wok and leave to cool.

3. Grind the nuts finely or crush them with a rolling pin.

4. Bring the water to the boil with sugar to taste and the salt. Add the almonds and stir in the cornflour. Simmer for 5 minutes and serve in small bowls after a large meal.

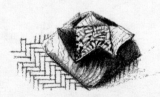

Sauces

1 Quick Sweet and Sour Sauce

Ingredients

1 large ripe tomato, quartered
100 g/4 oz/½ cup sugar
120 ml/4 fl oz/½ cup chicken stock
45 ml/3 tbsp white wine vinegar
15 ml/1 tbsp soy sauce
2.5 ml/½ tsp salt
15 ml/1 tbsp vegetable oil
3 gherkins, chopped
4 pieces preserved candied ginger, chopped
15 ml/1 tbsp cornflour
15 ml/1 tbsp water

Method

1. Place the tomato, sugar, stock, wine vinegar, soy sauce, salt and vegetable oil in a saucepan. Bring to the boil and simmer for 4 minutes, stirring continuously. Remove the tomato skin.

2. Add the gherkins and ginger. Blend the cornflour with the water and stir it into the sauce. Continue to cook, stirring for 4 minutes.

Makes about 450 ml/¾ pt/2 cups

2 Satay Sauce

Ingredients

100 g/4 oz/½ cup peanut butter
120 ml/4 fl oz/½ cup chicken stock
120 ml/4 fl oz/½ cup vegetable oil
15 ml/1 tbsp lemon juice
15 ml/1 tbsp soy sauce
2.5 ml/½ tsp salt
2.5 ml/½ tsp chilli powder
2.5 ml/½ tsp sugar

Method

1. Mix all the ingredients together thoroughly in a small saucepan over a low heat, stirring continuously. When the ingredients have all mixed together, remove from the heat and leave to cool.

2. Store in the refrigerator in an air-tight jar and stir well before using.

Makes about 375 ml/13 fl oz/1 ½ cups

Index